ANGRY CATHOLIC WOMEN

a sociological investigation
ANDREW M. GREELEY

a theological reflection
MARY G. DURKIN

THE THOMAS MORE PRESS

Chicago, Illinois

ISBN 0-88347-165-5

7152230

TABLE OF CONTENTS

INTRODUCTION

by Mary G. Durkin

In interdisciplinary study, when a process is fruitful, we tend to explore its use in further research. In a previous work (A Church To Come Home to, Thomas More Press, 1982) the authors of this present study examined how a process of pastoral theology must recognize the importance of religious experience and the influence of the religious imagination on this experience; this interdisciplinary approach to a pastoral theology also indicated some directions for church leaders and theologians who might want to address the increasing number of Catholics who are returning to the Church of their youth. We turn to this process again for the study of a particular segment of alienated Catholics—angry Catholic women—because we realize that a response to their anger based only on Church rules or doctrinal discussions will fall upon deaf ears. We hope that an investigation of the roots of this anger will provide some direction for theological reflection and pastoral response.

An early morning encounter in a mid-town Manhattan coffee shop and a conversation with a friend, a 1950's graduate of a Catholic woman's college, illustrate why there is a need for an interdisciplinary approach to the study of many of the issues confronting the Catholic religious community in the 1980's. After a concert and party a group of us, out-of-towners, stopped at an all night coffee shop empty save for the cook and waitress. A salesman, unable to sleep, also found our coffee shop an oasis in the wee hours of the morning. Perhaps attracted by the rather lively conversation of our group, he seated himself at an adjoining table and bantered with those adjacent to him. The conversation was fairly typical for strangers in a big city at that time of the morning--"Where are you from?" "What are you doing in New York?" and jokes about the quality of service in the coffee shop--until someone in our group mentioned "Catholic Church." Suddenly our stranger in the night, who had revealed a name that fit his Irish face, became a very angry man. We never discovered the cause of his anger, but we learned that, after sixteen years of Catholic education, he no longer considered himself a "practicing Catholic." He went to church when he felt like it, "not when some priest or pope tells me to go to church." He felt: "God will not send me to hell if I sleep late some Sunday morning because I've worked hard all week, and if God is really like that--if he will send me to hell--then I don't want to have anything to do with him." His children--he was a man in his early forties--were not forced to go to Mass but could go when they chose to.

Those in our group who were Catholic but did not share this man's obvious anger with the institutional church had no easy defense of the Church which could alleviate his anger. Theological arguments about the Church as the "people of God" or about the basic Catholic stance of hopefulness in a loving God would not erase strongly alienated feelings which were obviously rooted in past negative experiences of church. Our coffee shop companion needs a positive

4

experience of the Catholic Christian community, but until church leaders and pastoral workers have a deeper appreciation of the experience of religion in people's lives, we will be unable to respond to the anger of the alienated.

The conversation with the college classmate reinforced the conviction that, though theologians and church leaders and people familiar with the theology of the Second Vatican Council might welcome the new understanding of Church developed out of this theology, large numbers of Catholics are experiencing a religious turmoil at a level which is not affected by theological discussion or church mandates. My friend's anger seemed to be directed at an image of Church frozen in the 1950's. I could not specifically identify the source of her anger. However, after a reflection on our conversation I realized that my response--"You're talking about a Church that hasn't existed for twenty years"--was inadequate for the very real difficulty she was experiencing.

Yet those of us who have a professional interest in religion-- theologians, church leaders and pastoral workers--are trained to deal with rational discussion of theological issues and to minister to people within the structure of an organized church. We work for the Church, even when we have difficulties with specific persons or rules within the church structure, because we believe that the Church continues to proclaim the Good News of the Lord. We accept the inevitable limitations of the human, social institutional aspects of the Church, and we are able to correlate abstract theological discussion with our understanding of the experience of the modern world (and in some instances to reflect on our own personal religious experience). But, unfortunately, most of us fail to appreciate the influence that an experience of God—a religious experience either private or communal—has on a person's level of membership in an organized church. This failure to appreciate the importance of religious experience makes it difficult for us to understand the anger of the alienated Catholic and to respond to it both personally and professionally. So, too, our inability to recognize the impact of religious experience often leads us to ignore this important aspect of human experience in our reflection and pastoral planning.

In this work we will focus on the specific issue of anger among a segment of Catholic women. We begin with an analysis of the available sociological data looking specifically for an answer to the question: Why are some Catholic women angry with the Church while others from seemingly similar backgrounds are not? The sociological investigation of the first portion of this book reflects the conviction that religion is primarily imaginative behavior. We will understand and respond to the alienation of the salesman and of our Catholic college graduate when we appreciate the primacy of religious experience and the complexity of the formation of a religious imagination.

In this study we attempt to identify the factors which cause some Catholic women to perceive the Church as hostile to their search for meaning and so to withdraw from active participation in Church services. The complexity of the interplay of a variety of factors—feminism, education, confidence in church leadership, mothers, spouses, priests and image of God—to explain the "anger" of an alienated Catholic "feminist" reveals why abstract theological argumentation and church regulations are not sufficient to counter the negative experiences which have formed an image of the Church as hostile to a woman's search for meaning. Even when the argumentation is rooted in an attempt to relate to the modern world and the church regulations are updated to reflect the realities of contemporary life, they do not "speak" to the religious imagination.

The sociological evidence presents a challenge to theologians, church leaders and pastoral workers, because it emphasizes the double aspect of conversion. We who are professional church people will be able to respond to the anger of the alienated woman only when we permit ourselves to be "converted" to an appreciation of the importance of religious experience and religious imagination. The alienated Catholic woman might develop a more positive image of Church if she is offered an opportunity for a positive religious experience in which she is "converted" to a new image of Church. The theological response of the second portion of this book calls for continual interaction between theologians, church leaders and the pastoral worker all conscious of the "story" of angry Catholic women. Reflection on the sociological analysis leads to the conclusion that the theologian must attend to the development of a positive theology of sexuality and marriage. So, too, theology must gain an appreciation of femininity calling upon the rich images of our Catholic Christian tradition that might be vehicles for touching the religious imagination. In addition, the theologian needs to elaborate more fully a theology of the domestic church. In developing these theologies, the theologian needs to be in communication with pastoral workers and church leaders, drawing from them insights into the lives of individuals and church communities and nurturing in them a deeper understanding of the richness of the Catholic tradition and of the need for a pastoral theology which continually links religious experiences of individuals in religious community with the larger Christian tradition. The issues of 1) how the local church directly reinforces the religious imagination originally developed in the home and 2) the importance of pastoral leadership and lay responsibility in creating an environment for an experience of church as a supporter of woman's search for identity in the modern world also need our consideration.

Theologians approach sociological investigation and talk of religious imagination and religious experience somewhat warily and, when the focus of this particular investigation is the anger of a segment of Catholic women, theologians are even more reluctant to address the issue. The prospect of interdisciplinary study which might result in practical suggestions is probably unsettling to most scholars but especially to theologians who are most comfortable dealing with the rational, reflective aspects of religion, abstracting and generalizing about their subject matter. This tendency to abstract and generalize is carried over to the consideration of the subject of women where theologians are probably no different than the rest of humankind which tends to stereotype and generalize about all women. Ten years ago critics of my doctoral dissertation on a pastoral theology for upper middle class suburban women, felt the audience was too specific. The realization that there are specific groups within the Church, that there is a pluralism in the Church which must be addressed, is foreign to most theologians. So, too, the discussion of religious imagination and religious experience as it affects a group

8

of "angry" Catholic women demands a rethinking of <u>a priori</u> approaches to theological reflection. Yet the sociological evidence in this study demands that we be open to new approaches to theological reflection, a demand, unfortunately, most theologians assiduously ignore.

This interdisciplinary study does not root our reflection and rational discussion only in the evidence of a particular time and culture. Rather, in our theological reflection, we attempt to uncover ways to enrich both our theological reflection and the experience of religion rooted in contemporary culture through an interaction between these various aspects of the all-encompassing experience of religion. In the process we hope to shed some light on how social scientist, theologian, church leader and pastoral worker might work together to enrich both the experience of religion at its primary level and the understanding of religion at the more abstract level. Specifically, we will see how an investigation of the anger of a certain group of Catholic women causes us to dig more deeply into the riches of our Catholic Christian tradition to alleviate that anger, seeking to avoid a continuation of circumstances which will nurture that anger in succeeding generations.

This interdisciplinary study of one manifestation of the influence of religious imagination on religious behavior is only a beginning step in what needs to be an ongoing process if we want to understand the complexity of circumstances which contribute to religious behavior (including that of those who study this behavior). Just as theologians can find their theological reflection enriched by acknowledgement of the importance of religious imagination, church leaders and pastoral workers could experience more fruitful results

9

from their labors if their efforts are geared to addressing those aspects of a person's life which most deeply affect their religious behavior. This study of angry Catholic women seeks to contribute to an understanding of religious behavior.

SOCIOLOGICAL ANALYSIS

by Andrew M. Greeley

CHAPTER I: OVERVIEW

The present essay is a study of "anger" towards the Roman Catholic Church among some of its women members. Since the study is an exercise in empirical data analysis, the terms must be defined precisely. "Anger" means a negative correlation between church attendance and certain attitudes about the participation of women in political, economic and religious life. It will be argued in the present essay that this problem of "anger" is limited to Catholics and Baptists in American society and that among both groups it relates to the low level of confidence in church leadership. Moreover, Roman Catholic women's "anger" seems to result from the images of Church and Woman they acquired from their mothers during their childhood years.

In terms of the illumination it may shed on the present ambiguity of the relationship between organized religion and women, the analysis undertaken has one very considerable advantage and a number of disadvantages.

The advantage is the analysis will be based on solid empirical evidence, not sweeping and undocumented generalizations. One will not be able to say, on the basis of this report that "Catholic women are angry at the Church." Rather, one will be able to say much more precisely, that some Catholic women are angry at the Church because they apparently perceive the Church as wishing to limit them to old, narrowly defined gender roles, and one will be able to make this assertion with considerable confidence.

The disadvantages of the present investigation are the following:

1. The project engages in "secondary" analysis, i.e., it uses existing data files—NORC's annual General Social Survey and a 1979 study of young Catholic adults—to answer research questions instead of generating new data collection. It does not follow, as an incompetent nun argued once in a review in the <u>National Catholic News Service</u>, that the analysis, because "secondary", is therefore "invalid." In both cases, the data are based on representative national samples and the analysis is perfectly valid. It does follow, however, that some information which would be useful for the analysis is simply unavailable because the appropriate questions were not included in the original primary research. Obviously it would be desirable to study the situation of women in the Catholic Church from the point of view of a research project which was designed specifically with that goal in mind and which asked a variety of questions to be dictated by such an interest. However, until such a project is funded (and don't anyone hold their breath!) secondary analysis is a useful and valid though somewhat limited technique for understanding the problems of women in the Roman Catholic Church.

2. "Feminism" is defined herein merely to mean for young women an agreement with the proposition that "it is important to allow women to become priests" and a disagreement with the proposition that "a pre-school child is likely to suffer emotional damage if the mother works." The women in the General Social Survey who are categorized as "feminists" are in disagreement with the propositions that "most men are better suited for politics than are most women" and

"women should take care of running their homes and leave running the country up to men" and in agreement with the proposition that "it is all right for a married woman to earn money in business or industry if she has a husband capable of supporting her."

At first glance, these five measures of "feminism" seem distressingly moderate. Militant Feminists would consider such propositions a very mild beginning of "raised consciousness." And yet, in fact, only about two-fifths of the young Catholic women in the 1979 study agree that women should be priests and disagree that a child will suffer emotional harm if her mother works and only approximately two-fifths of all women in America (Catholics slightly more likely than Protestants) think that it's all right for a women to work even if her husband earns enough money and that women are as qualified for politics as men and women ought not to leave the running of the country to men. Thus, even though "feminism" in the present report is severely limited and mildly expressed, it nonetheless attracts less than half of the populations being studied. Doubtless there is another Feminism among Catholic women-- including for example, private celebration by women of "eucharistic" services, with a wide-ranging, clearly articulated and ideologically consistent set of attitudes. About this Feminism the present report is able to say nothing. Compared to it, the "feminism" I am describing may seem like the "green wood."

Ecclesiastical leaders and policy makers might ponder after reading this essay that if things are so bad in the green wood, they must have even more serious problems in the dry wood. But it would not be appropriate to conclude, from my analysis, that the same dynamics that are at work among the "feminists" in this report also apply to Feminists.

3. Any empirical data analysis is necessarily intricate and qualified. Those who search this book for sweeping generalizations about the relationship between women and Roman Catholicism will necessarily be disappointed. Moreover, they may also be offended that, in the face of what they may take to be terrible injustice to women, I am content to submit what may seem to be a cautious, careful and restrained report. They also may be disturbed that in seeking an explanation for "anger" among Catholic "feminists" in their childhood experiences, I am "blaming" the victim, i.e., "blaming" women for being angry at the Church when their anger is not only appropriate but perhaps too mild.

However, it is the responsibility of the social researcher to be cautious and precise and pedestrian in his work, whatever his own personal feelings and convictions might be. Moreover, it is the function of the researcher not to "blame" but to seek to understand. I am a "feminist" by the standards of this report (which would make be one of a minority of American Catholic men; indeed, a minority of Catholic men who are still under 30 years old). Moreover, I am also a Feminist and deeply disturbed by the discrimination against women in the Church (and all other human institutions) and vigorously support the appropriate social changes. Nonetheless, I feel that if church leadership is to deal adequately with the problems it faces, it must understand the depth and complexity of these problems. The anger about which this essay is written is a deep and complicated anger and will not be resolved easily or simply. When I locate much of the problem of the anger in the imaginations of the respondents, particularly as these imaginations were shaped by experiences of Church and Woman in their childhood, I am not blaming anyone but rather trying to illuminate complicated causes of the disenchantment with the Church of a certain fairly good-sized proportion of its population.

I do not consider one of the disadvantages of the present project to be that this is undertaken by a male researcher. I deem it prejudice to say that a man is incapable of carrying out a useful and objective analysis of the problem under consideration. I also deem it foolish for such a male analyst to think that he would have all the insights necessary to make the most of the present analysis and not need the help of the insights of women scholars who are his colleagues. I have availed myself of the insights and suggestions of a number of women colleagues but I refuse to take seriously or even to discuss the argument that this analysis is irrelevant or invalid because it has been done by a man. In fact, as our evidence demonstrates, men over thirty are more likely to be "feminists" than are women over thirty and I am rather decidedly over thirty. My theological sibling contributed a commentary and reflection on the data analysis because such a contribution seemed to both of us to be important and useful and not to fend off the bigotry of angry ideologues who aren't to be listened to, whether they be Male Chauvinists or Female Chauvinists.

The theoretical context for this report results from my conviction that religion in both its origins and power is primarily imaginative behavior, rooted in experiences which intermittently renew human hope, retained in the memory as interpreted images (symbols) and shared with others in stories that recount the experiences which have renewed hope and given direction and purpose to life and to explain metaphorically what life means. In such a perspective, the reflective and rational dimension aspects of religion are important and indeed essential but are derivative rather than primary (for much more detailed development of this theoretical perspective, see my books Religion: A Secular Theory and The Religious Imagination). In such a perspective, one expects that one may be able to find an explanation of the "anger" in certain Catholic women in terms of daily life experiences with the Church and Woman which are incompatible with their current "feminist" convictions. The lower level of church attendance may be explicable in terms of this imaginative incompatibility.

It might perhaps be useful to rephrase the question from the opposite perspective: how can "feminism" be compatible with church attendance? For while "feminists" are less likely to go to Church regularly than not "feminists," still many of them do go to Church regularly. Perhaps one might suggest that they "ought" to demonstrate their dissatisfaction with the Church by staying away from frequent Mass attendance but they don't, and that needs to be explained.

From the perspective of my theory of religion as imaginative behavior, it could be explained by the fact that for one reason or another, these church-going "feminists" see no incompatibility between religious devotion and their feminist convictions. The reason for such a non-perception of incompatibility is that they do not "imagine" the Church in the same way as do the non-devout "feminists."

The Church, as John Kotre pointed out in his book <u>On the Border</u>, is a complex and multi-faceted phenomenon which emits many different signals. Which of the signals one chooses to focus on is, as Kotre points out, likely to be a function of one's own personality as a signal receiving mechanism. One might tentatively suggest at the beginning of this essay that the devout "feminists" have very different images of church than the non-devout "feminists" and then ask "whence come these different images?"

CHAPTER II: DATA

Approximately half of the young Catholics in the United States
(in a survey conducted in 1979) approve of either the ordination of
women and working mothers (Table 1.1) and approximately one-fourth
of the men and one-third of the women approve of both. Moreover
(Table 1.2) the not "feminists" are half again as likely (47% as opposed to 30%) to attend church regularly. It is this 17 percentage
point difference in church attendance which constitutes the analytic
challenge to the present report. Why do attitudes which might be tak-
en to stand against traditional gender role definition lead to lower
levels of church attendance for Catholic women? (As we will see sub-
sequently, such attitudes do not lead to lower levels of church attendance for members of most American protestant denominations.)

To project from the sample to the Catholic population between 18
and 30, there are a little more than six million young Catholic women
between 18 and 30. Two million of them would be, by our definition,
"feminists;" 17% of that two million would be approximately 340,000
young women who are not attending Church regularly because they
believe women should be ordained and it's proper for mothers of young
children to work. I hardly need observe that, for a Church which has
spoken repeatedly in recent years about the need to "evangelize,"
this very large number of alienated young women represents a
significant evangelistic challenge.

The "feminists" are not significantly different in many respects
from other young Catholic women (Table 1.2A). Their rating of the
sermons, of the sympathy of priests' attitudes towards lay people,

even of the desirability of their daughter being a nun are not significantly different than the attitudes of the not "feminists." They are also not different from the not "feminists" in their recollections of a happy childhood and the reports of a happy and sexually fulfilled marriage. They are significantly more likely to approve abortion if a mother wants no more children (24 percentage points more likely, in fact) and also significantly more likely (18 percentage points) to approve of living together before marriage. Moreover, the "feminists" are substantially less likely to say that they have a great deal of confidence in church leadership, though the way the question is worded—"as far as the people running these institutions are concerned, how much confidence do you have in them" on the response "organized religion," the women might, in fact, be answering about all religious leaders and not just Catholic religious leaders. As we shall see in a subsequent chapter, however, it is only for Catholics and Baptists that attitudes towards church leaders seems to be a mediating variable between "feminism" and lower levels of church attendance).

Table 1.3 is the typical table which will be used in this report—the "model" if you will, for our analysis. It shows differences in regular church attendance between "feminists" and not "feminists." The relationship between "feminism" and church attendance we have defined for the purposes of this report as "anger." It could also be called "alienation." The goal of our analysis will be either to eliminate the differences and thus "explain" why the "feminists" are less likely to go to Church or, failing that, to "specify" the difference, i.e., to indicate what subsegments of the population of Catholic women are the ones in which the "anger" or "alienation" is likely to be found.

Table 1.3 is a specification (as will be virtually all of the tables in the present report). There is no significant difference in church attendance between the "feminists" and not "feminists" who have a great deal of confidence in church leadership but there is a significant difference in church attendance between the "feminists" and not "feminists" for those who have less than "a great deal of confidence" in those running organized religion. Thus, for the question of why do some "feminists" go to Church as often as not "feminists" do—the beginning of an answer is that "feminists" go to Church if they have, despite their "feminism," a great deal of confidence in church leadership.

("Significant" is used in this essay in the narrow statistical sense of the word. It refers to the chance—always less than 1 in 20 —that the relationship which exists in the sample will not also exist in the general population.)

Might the image of Church and intense attitudes towards church leaders be affected by whether a young woman has attended college? Clearly (Table 1.4) college attendance has a considerable effect. There is not a statistically significant difference in church attendance between the "feminists" and the not "feminists" but there is (23 percentage points) for those who have attended college. If one combines confidence in church leadership and college attendance one finds that the statistically significant negative relationship between "feminism" and church attendance is confined to those who have lower levels of confidence in religious leadership and who have attended college. In this specified subsegment of the young Catholic woman population, the "feminists" are only half as likely to go to church as the not "feminists" (20 percentage points versus 40 percentage points). What eliminates the likelihood of a "feminist" being less devout than a not "feminist?" Both non-college attendance and a great deal of confidence in church leaders seem to eliminate the negative relationship. If one wishes to discover the reasons for the "anger" of some young Catholic women, one must concentrate on those who attended college and who have something less than a great deal of confidence in religious leadership.

Another way of describing this "specification" or "localization" is presented in Table 1.6. Using the "B" statistic in a series of multiple egression equations, one can account for the 17 percentage point difference in church attendance between "feminists" and not "feminists." If one takes into consideration merely the higher level of confidence in church leadership among the not "feminists," the difference is diminished from 17 percentage points to 13 percentage points. If one then takes into account the interaction between "feminism" and education ("feminists" are more likely to attend college) the difference declines to 12 percentage points; and if, finally, one takes into account the interaction between education and confidence in church leadership (the educated have less confidence in church leadership), the difference becomes statistically insignificant. The interplay of "feminism," education and confidence in church leadership constitutes the raw material for an explanation of why "feminists" are one-third less likely to attend Church regularly than not "feminists." One must concentrate on the better educated and more "anti-clerical" segment of the young Catholic population if one wishes to understand more about the "anger" of young "feminist" Catholics towards their Church.

CHAPTER III: "FEMINISM" AND MOTHERS

The theoretical perspective of this report on the importance of
the religious imagination has led us to expect that the images of
Church and religion from a woman's childhood experience might explain the negative relationship between religious devotion and "feminism." Unfortunately, we have only a limited number of variables
available which give us information about our respondents' childhood
experiences. One of them, however, is very important since it addresses itself directly to the question of whether the pre-school
child of a working mother is emotionally harmed and that is the question of whether the respondent's mother worked when she was a pre-
school child (whether the mother worked at later times in the young
woman's life was also asked in the survey and had no effect at all
on the analysis herein reported). Might it not be that those college
educated "feminists" whose mothers actually worked during the respondent's pre-school period and would therefore have been expected to
have had an image of "feminist" behavior available to them would be
even more angered at the Church's opposition (as they perceived it)
to the elimination of old gender roles and hence even less likely to
attend Church?

Or might it not be the other way around? Might not such young
women have learned from the example of their mothers that "feminism"
and religion are compatible and hence see no conflict in their adult
life between Woman and Church because the images inherited from their
childhood experience are not incompatible?

Table 2.1 provides strong evidence for the second possibility. If the mother of a college educated respondent worked when the respondent was under six, there was no statistically significant reason to expect that "feminism" would lead to lower levels of church attendance. However, it is precisely among those respondents who attended college and whose mothers did not work during the first six years of the respondent's life that one finds a significant and indeed dramatic difference in church attendance between the "feminists" and the not "feminists." The former are approximately one-third as likely to attend church as the latter. The "anger" which is the object of our study seems to be specified, i.e., localized, in precisely that population group of college educated women who did not have available an image of a working mother to assure the compatibility of images of Woman and Church if the respondent is now committed to "feminist" positions.

And (Table 2.2) it is again precisely in this population category that the lack of confidence in church leadership has its effect. "Feminism," in other words, leads to lower levels of religious devotion when all of the following are true: the respondent went to college; the respondent does not have a great deal of confidence in church leaders; the respondent's mother did not work during the first six years of the respondent's life. If the image of Woman that one has acquired as a "feminist," to put the matter differently, is incompatible with the image of Woman acquired in childhood and the latter image is attributed to the Church, the present adult respondent feels conflict between Modern Woman and Church and therefore has lower levels of confidence in church leadership and is less likely to attend

Church regularly. There are four forces at work in this incompatibility: image of Woman perceived as child; image of Church perceived as child; image of Woman as influenced by "feminism" and enhanced by college education; and image of Church in the present. The present images are incompatible because the present image of Church is identified with the image of Church one acquired in childhood and that in turn is identified with the image of Woman acquired in childhood and that image in its turn is incompatible with the image of Woman as defined by "feminist" principles. The attached graph demonstrates the compatibility and incompatibility of images (Figure 2.1)

The nature of our data makes it impossible to put parameters on the lines in Figure 2.1, but it is possible to examine the relationships among images of Woman and Church for both "feminist" and "traditional" women. Thus, one would hypothesize that for the "traditional" (Figure 2.2) that all three relationships will be positive—if you are not a "feminist" and if you're mother did not work and went to Church regularly, then you will be much more likely to attend Church regularly.

Indeed such is the case, though the expected positive relationship between a non-working mother and church attendance is rather weak.

On the other hand, one would expect just the opposite for the "feminists"—a negative relationship between traditional images of woman and church and current Mass attendance. The expectation is sustained, though the negative relationship between mother's church attendance and respondent's is not statistically significant. However,

26

the difference between the two groups on the top line is .31 and on the bottom is .24, indicating a very different dynamic at work, a difference in dynamic which our theory would have led us to expect. The same point can be made by the regression equation results presented in Table 2.3. There is a 23 percentage point difference among college educated Catholic young women in the church attendance of the "feminists" and not "feminists." If the interaction between mother's work and "feminism" is put into the equation, the difference is reduced to 3 percentage points; and then if a second interaction between "feminism" and confidence in church leadership is introduced into the equation, the sign is reversed and there becomes a positive relationship between "feminism" and church attendance. The interaction then, among the variables--"feminism," mother's work and confidence in church leadership--explains the difference in church attendance between "feminists" and not "feminists" who went to college.

The conflict between "feminist" positions and the contemporary Church, in other words, a conflict manifested in lower levels of church attendance, is in fact rooted in the young woman's past experiences and images and is, in some sense, a function of a conflict she perceives between her own image of Woman and the image of Woman she observed in her mother. The Church, which was seen as endorsing and perhaps, indeed, causing her mother's image of Woman is now perceived as still endorsing that image and necessarily at odds with the young adult woman's image of Woman. The present Church, in other words, is suffering from the identification of a past image of Church with a childhood image of Woman.

On the other hand, those young women, who are "feminists" and who perceive "feminism" as compatible with an image of Woman absorbed from their past (because their mother worked when they were small children) are not offended by the past image of Church and hence are not offended by the present image of Church . They therefore see no incompatibility between their image of Church and image of Woman and are as likely to go to Church weekly as are not "feminists."

CHAPTER IV: "FEMINISM," MOTHER'S DEVOTION & CLOSENESS TO GOD

The weak link in the image incompatibility explanation portrayed in Figure 2.1, as many readers will doubtless have perceived, is that thus far I have been unable to establish that the Catholic "feminists" who do not go to Church in fact attribute the image of Woman they observed in their mothers to the Church. Thus far I have not established the compatibility of the image of Church and the image of Mother in the previous generation which creates among college-educated "feminists" whose mothers did not work incompatibility between the image of Church and the image of Woman in the present generation.

However, the specification depicted in Table 3.1 does strongly suggest that in the mind of the young "feminist" the traditional image of Woman they observed in their mothers is indeed linked to an image of Church. A statistically significant difference in church attendance (one of almost 40 percentage points) exists only for those college educated women whose mothers did not work during the first six years of their life and whose mothers attend Church every week. Though the number of cases are obviously very limited in this microanalysis, it would appear that if a woman's mother did not attend Church every week, i.e, if she were not very devout, then the woman does not link the image of Woman from her childhood with an image of Church from her childhood. If, on the other hand, the mother was both traditional in church attendance and traditional in her exercise of the role of Woman, then those two traditionalities are linked and if her daughter is a "feminist," then the daughter's "feminism" will have a negative impact on her church attendance. The problem for the Church in the present, in other words, has been created precisely because, for the mother of our respondent, there was a high degree of compatibility between religious devotion and traditional of the role of Woman. When the daughter dissents from the one, there is a propensity for her dissent from the other.

Finally, our theory of religious imagination leads us to believe that one fact which can cancel out propensity to stay away from Church is a response to the image of God.

To put the matter succinctly, the incompatibility of images of Woman and Church can be eliminated if a respondent has a powerful image of God, since God is (despite the behavior of many leaders of the Roman Catholic Church) more important than the Church. While the numbers of respondents in Table 3.2 are small, it is nonetheless the case that the statistically significant difference in church attendance between "feminists" and not "feminists" (a difference of 40 percentage points) among those respondents who went to college, whose mothers did not work, whose mothers attended Mass every week, is to be found precisely among those respondents who do not feel extremely or very close to God. In other words, if you feel close to God, then the incompatibility of your present image of Woman with the image of Woman in your childhood and your image of Church seems to be eliminated. While you may "blame" the Church for the image of Woman with which you were raised and which you now reject, that blame does not keep you away from church attendance because you still like God and you feel that God likes you. God, in other words, becomes a suppressor variable!

The complex relationship among the images of God, Woman, and Church for those who went to college but whose mothers did not work while they were under six years of age, is illustrated in the results of the regression equations that are presented in Table 3.3. There are 30 percentage points difference in church attendance in this sub-population between "feminists" and not "feminists." The difference diminishes to 20 percentage points when one takes into account confidence in church leadership and mother's church attendance and then to statistical insignificance when one takes into account two interactions--one between "feminism" and mother's Mass attendance and the other between "feminism" and Closeness to God. In other words, to explain the differences in church devotion between the two groups (for those who went to college and whose mothers did not work) one has to take into account their contemporary image of Church, their image of Church in their mother's generation, their image of Woman in their mother's generation (as shaped by the fact that their mothers did not work when they were young) and their present image of God. Figure 3.1 is an approximation of how the system we are describing might work. There is still an incompatibility between current image of Woman and childhood image of Woman. Childhood image of Woman is still compatible with childhood image of Church but the contemporary image of Church is not affected either by childhood image of Church or childhood image of Woman because an image of God intervenes to suppress these links and the resulting incompatibilities between current image of Church and current image of Woman.

The importance of religious imagery for "cancelling" "feminist" anger can be illustrated if one modifies the analytic paradigm somewhat, considers only "feminists," and asks what effect an image of God has on a variable that predicts Mass attendance for "feminists" or predicts Mass attendance in the rest of the population.

Thus, it has been argued that "feminists" whose mothers worked are more likely to attend church services frequently because the image of Church and the image of Woman in their childhood were not linked in such a way as to set up antagonism in later life between image of Church and image of Woman. This finding is illustrated in Table 3.4 which shows that the "feminists" who are daughters of working mothers are more likely to go to Church than the "feminists" who are not daughters of working mothers. Perhaps the reason for this might be that the daughters of the working mothers might have somewhat less traditional images of God than the daughters of non-working mothers. Table 3.5 offers persuasive evidence for this line of reasoning. The image of God as "Lover" (proportion extremely likely to imagine God as "Lover") has no effect at all on the church attendance of "feminists" whose mothers did not work but a powerful impact on the church attendance of "feminists" whose mothers did work during the first six years of their daughters lives.

A non-traditional image of God and of God as "Lover" is the seventh in frequency out of eight possible images (only God as "Mother" is less likely to be described as an "extremely likely" imaginative response to the word God) and has no effect at all on the church attendance of those "feminists" who, by their mothers' behavior, might be expected to have an image of Woman that was traditional. However, if this link between traditional Woman and traditional Church is broken by the fact the daughter had a non-traditional image of Woman because her mother worked for the first six years of her life, the non-traditional image of God as "Lover" has an enormous effect on the church attendance, increasing the proportion of "feminists" going to Church regularly to 69%. Even though the number of respondents in each of the cells in Table 3.5 is small, nonetheless, among those "feminists" whose mothers did work during the first six years of their life, the image of God as "Lover" does have a significant effect on their church attendance. The open image of Woman from their childhood, in other words, prepares the way for a non-traditional image of God to produce an extremely favorable image of Church while in a family in which the Mother followed the traditional image of Woman, the "feminist" daughter is simply immune to the impact of the non-traditional image of God.

A similar phenomenon is at work if one considers the effect of Mother's church attendance for not "feminists," i.e., there is a fairly strong link between mother's church attendance and daughter's. However, for "feminists" (Table 3.6) mothers' church attendance has no effect at all on daughter's church attendance. The non-traditional image (Table 3.7) of God as "Lover" is able to have a substantial and statistically significant impact on the "feminist" daughter's church attendance if her mother was not devout (while it does not have any effect at all on the church attendance of the "feminist" daughter of a devout mother). Breaking the link between the image of God and the image of either Church or Woman enables a non-traditional (but very powerful) image of God to incline a "feminist" toward a dramatically benign image of Church and indeed to be extremely devout.

To repeat, the last four tables are based on a very small number of cases, but the differences are statistically significant in Tables 3.5 and 3.7 and they are counter-intuitive, i.e., one would have expected, if one were not using the theory of the religious imagination that is guiding this analysis, that the image of God as "Lover" would cancel out the negative effects of "feminism" for young women from both devout and traditional backgrounds. In fact, just the opposite occurs: the powerful image of God as "Lover" is able not merely to cancel out but to dramatically reverse the relationship between "feminism" and church attendance only when something in the young woman's past cracked the ordinary link between traditional role models and traditional piety.

Figures 3.2 and 3.3 put, as best we can, parameters on the lines in Figure 3.1 and illustrate the patterns described in the previous paragraphs. The God as "Lover" image does not significantly correlate with Mass attendance for "traditional" women but does so correlate for "feminist" women--a finding which could not have been anticipated unless one was thinking in terms of religious experiences and images, both traditional and non-traditional.

The picture of God in one's imagination, in other words, exorcises the incompatibilities between the image of Church in the past and the image of Woman in the present. The image of God, if not a deus ex machina, then at least is a deus in machina. How much work there is for a deity to do in the machine can be illustrated by the specifications in Table 3.4. Of the whole sample of young adults, the not "feminists" are only 12 percentage points more likely to go to church than the "feminists." Among women, the difference rises to 17 percentage points. Among college educated women, the difference increases to 22 percentage points. Among college educated women whose mothers did not work, the difference is 30 percentage points and among college women whose mothers did not work but were devout church goers, the difference is 37 percentage points. Finally, when the difference is limited to college educated women whose devout mothers did not work and who did not themselves feel close to God, the difference is 40 percentage points--almost 3-1/2 times as high as it is in the general population. The complex interplay of imagery--Woman, Church, Self, Mother and God--is required to understand why some Catholic "feminists" do go to church regularly and some do not.

CHAPTER V: CATHOLIC WOMEN IN THE GENERAL SOCIAL SURVEY

In the previous three chapters, we have explored the relationship between "feminism" and church attendance for Catholics between
18 and 30 and developed an explanation based on incompatibility of imagery to account for the difference in church attendance between
young "feminists" and young not "feminists". Data collected in the
National Opinion Research Center's annual General Social Survey
(which has asked "feminist" questions five times during the last ten
years) enables us to look at all Catholic women and, indeed, at women
who belong to other religious denominations to supplement and perhaps
develop the explanation presented in the last three sections.   During
the 1970's, there was no significant difference between Catholic men
and Catholic women in their attitudes towards the role of women as
measured by our three items; however, in the 1982 General Social
Survey, while both men and women became more likely to endorse all
three of our propositions and indeed, the men in 1982 were as pro
"feminist" as were the women in the 1970's.   The very substantial increase (some 43% to 57%) among women created for the first time in
1982 a significant difference between women and men in the proportion
that is "feminist."

Moreover, (Table 4.4) while both among men and women the proportion of "feminists" increases the younger a respondent is, it is only
among people under 40 that the proportion of "feminism" is notably
higher for women than for men. Interestingly enough, among those in
their twenties, (approximately the same age as those interviewed in
the 1979 study) the gap between women and men diminishes because the

youngest men seem to be catching up to their women counterparts. Thus, among people in their fifties and older, 43% of the men and 22% of the women are "feminists," giving the men a distinct advantage; whereas among those in their twenties, 49% of the men and 59% of the women are "feminists."

In the General Social Survey population there is a statistically significant difference in church attendance between "feminist" women and not "feminists" of 14 percentage points; approximately the same difference reported in the previous chapters, while there is no significant difference in church attendance between "feminist" men and not "feminist" men.

Women under thirty in the General Social Survey are roughly equivalent in age to the women interviewed in the Knights of Columbus study, and as Table 4.5 demonstrates, the relationship between church attendance and "feminism" and college education is approximately the same. If the respondent under thirty in the General Social Survey did not go to college and she is a "feminist," she is not significantly less likely to go to church than her not "feminist" counterparts. However, if she attended college there is a significant difference, indeed of 36 percentage points in the average church attendance of the not "feminists" when compared to the "feminists." However, college education does not seem to play the same role for women over 30 in specifying "feminist" attitudes as it does for those under 30, so the analysis reported in this section takes a slightly different course.

The first question to be asked is whether the mother's employment before the respondent was six has the same effect on the relationship between "feminism" and church attendance for the whole population of Catholic women as it did on the young women discussed in the previous three sections. And, indeed, the same phenomenon does appear to be at work. While there is not a significant difference between "feminists" and not "feminists" in church attendance if the mother worked before the child was six, there is a significant 19 percentage point difference in church attendance between "feminists" and the not "feminists" if the mother did not work. Daughters of working mothers are less likely to go to church than the daughters of non-working mothers, but their "feminism" has no effect on their church attendance in the former case and a considerable effect on the latter case. The incompatibility of Woman as reflected by Mother and of Woman as experienced by Daughter does not seem to be limited just to young Catholics, although college does not play the role in the incompatibility for older women that it did for younger women.

Moreover, again it is among those who lack a great deal of confidence in church leadership (Table 4.6) that one finds statistically significant differences among all Catholic women between the "feminists" and the not "feminists" in their religious devotion.

Because we have in the General Social Survey information on the work force status of women respondents, we are able to ask whether it is the working woman or the non-working woman who is more likely to be angry at the Church. Perhaps the working woman would be more angry because she might perceive herself as violating the Church's preferred gender role models.

Or perhaps the non-working woman would be more angry at the Church because she can blame the Church, i.e., the image of Church she absorbed as a child for the fact that she is not working and is dissatisfied with her situation (Tables 4.7 to 4.13 explore this possibility).

A woman was defined as "housewife" if she was not working full time; even those who were working part-time were placed in the "housewife" category because it turned out, in preliminary analysis, that the phenomenon to be described differentiates between full-time working women and all other women.

Indeed, it is the non-working woman, i.e., the housewives, who are likely to be "angry" at the Church. The working woman (the "non-housewife")is less likely to go to Church than the housewife but her "feminism" has no statistically significant impact on the likelihood that she will go to church whereas there is an 18 percentage point difference between the "feminist" housewives and the not "feminist" housewives in their church attendance. It is those who stay at home, and who are nonetheless "feminists," who are less likely to go to Church.

The happiness of one's own marriage does not affect the negative relationship between "feminism" and church attendance (Table 4.7), but low levels of satisfaction with one's family situation do (Tables 4.8 and 4.9), and the relationship is specified (Table 4.10) as existing only for those housewives who are less than very satisfied with their family situation. It is not, then, the quality of relationship between husband and wife that contributes to the alienation from church devotion but a more generalized dissatisfaction with one's family situation which presumably means that, even though one is a "feminist," one is not able to practice one's "feminist" principles by seeking employment.

There is also a propensity to invoke the image of the Church in this explanation; the statistically significant differences (almost 30 percentage points) between "feminist" and not "feminist" in church attendance occur only among those housewives with low family satisfaction who, in addition, are less than very confident in church leadership. There is, then, in this total Catholic population, incompatibility between image of Church and image of Woman which is heightened by the dissatisfaction of the woman between her own image of Woman and the actuality of her experience as Woman. Finally, just as for young Catholics as reported in the previous three chapters and for Catholics between 18 and 30 as described in Table 4.5 in the present chapter, whether one's mother worked when one was a child under six has a considerable and a statistically significant impact on the relationship. If the mother worked when one was under six , there is no correlation between "feminism" and church attendance. If the mother did not work, however, the not "feminist" is half again as likely to attend weekly church as the "feminist."

Even though the number of cases again are severely limited (Table 4.13), it is precisely the image of Mother that specified the difference between "feminists" and not "feminists" in a statistically significant way among dissatisfied housewives. Even though a woman is not presently working and she is dissatisfied with her family situation, as long as her mother worked before she was six, there will not be a significant correlation between "feminism" and church attendance.

If one is dissatisfied and a housewife, there is a 40 percentage points difference in church attendance between the "feminists" and the not "feminists" if the mother did not work before the respondent was six. An image of Woman from the past compatible with one's "feminist" image of Woman in the present protects the Church from incompatibility with the current image of Woman, even if one is dissatisfied with one's family situation. Figure 4.1 illustrates the suggested patterns of image relationships. Being a housewife is compatible with both present and past image of the Church and also with the past image of Woman but is incompatible with the present image of Woman. Thus, as closeness to God in the previous chapter diminished and indeed eliminated the antagonism between current image of Woman and the image of Church so the image of housewife enhances the incompatibility. The dissatisfied housewife with one image of Woman from her childhood and another image in the present, if she is a "feminist," finds that her present image of Woman is incompatible with her childhood image of Church. This incompatibility reinforces the negative relationship between her current image of Woman and her current image of Church. If, on the other hand, there is compatibility between present image of Woman and childhood image of Woman, the present image of Church does not suffer even if the woman is a dissatisfied feminist housewife. Unfortunately, we have no data on mother's church attendance in the General Social Survey. Hence, we cannot say quite so confidently that traditional religious devotion and traditional views of women were indeed blended into one over-arching im-

41

age which is incompatible for the "feminists" with current image of Woman. Nonetheless, there does not seem to be any reason to doubt that linkage.

(Subsequent NORC General Social Surveys will ask about religious devotion.)

Finally, two interactions between "feminism" and family satisfaction and between family and confidence in church leadership do account for all of the 14 percentage points difference in church attendance in the general population of Catholic women between "feminists" and not "feminists." "Feminists" are less likely to attend Church because they are more dissatisfied with their present situation and because they have less confidence in church leadership. The differences are localized among the dissatisfied and the non-confident. Combining the mutually reinforcing analyses of data from two independent samples, one could summarize by the following observation: The "anger" of Catholic "feminists" is the result of conflict among images of the Church, past and present, Woman, past and present, and God and Housewife, present.

If the present Church is, for one reason or another, linked to the past image of Woman, then only a strong image of God can protect the Church from anger. If, on the other hand, the link between the present Church and the past image of Woman is reinforced by the present image of Dissatisfied Housewife, then the incompatibility between present Church and present Woman, an incompatibility which results in lower levels of religious devotion, is reinforced. Church leadership trying to intervene in this image system will discover that the image of Church is caught up in conflicting images of Mother, Real Self and Ideal Self. It will be a delicate system of images to challenge.

On the other hand, the fact that somewhere between a 1,000,000 and 1,500,000 Catholic women do not attend church regularly precisely because of this complex interplay of imagery is one from which responsible church leadership can hardly turn away.

CHAPTER VI: DENOMINATIONS AND POLITICS

Catholics are neither the most "feminist" nor least "feminist" American religious group. Catholic women are more likely to
be "feminists" than are Baptists, Methodists, and Lutheran women as
well as "other" Protestant women but less likely to be "feminists"
than Jews, Episcopalians, and respondents with no denominational af-
filiation (Table 5.1, which is based on data drawn from the NORC
General Social Survey). Catholic men, in addition to lagging behind
Episcopalians and Jews, are somewhat less likely to be "feminists"
than are Lutherans or Presbyterians but more likely than are
Methodists and Baptists.

However, among those denominations which are large enough to
have enough respondents in the five General Social Surveys used in
this analysis, there are no statistically significant relationships
between "feminism" and church attendance among Methodists or
Lutherans or Presbyterian women (Table 5.2). But Baptists, like
Catholics, display a substantial difference in religious observance
between "feminist" and not "feminists," a difference which (Table
5.3) is specified as precisely occurring among those Baptists who
have low levels of confidence in religious leadership. However, none
of the variables that seem to account for the differences between
"feminists" and not "feminists" in the Catholic population (besides
the lack of confidence in church leadership) appear to have any impact at all on "anger" among Baptists. The results may be the same
for Catholics and Baptists, but it would appear the dynamics

producing the results are different and will require further analysis in the years to come.

The anger of "feminists" towards their church is not something that is to be found in all American denominations. Although Roman Catholics do not have a monopoly on it, there are other denominations in which the image incompatibility we have discussed in this essay simply does not seem to exist, quite possibly because childhood images of Church and of Woman are not perceived by members of these other denominations as being incompatible with present images of Woman.

Catholic women "feminists" do not seem to be subscribing to a coherent liberal party line (Table 5.4). Indeed, Independents are more likely to be "feminists" than either Democrats or Republicans regardless of whether one describes oneself as liberal or moderate or conservative (Table 5.4). Liberal Democrats, liberal Republicans, conservative Democrats and conservative Republicans do not differ greatly from one another in the proportion that are "feminists," whereas liberal and conservative Independents are the ones where the "feminist" position is most likely to occur, and moderates are less likely to be "feminists" than either liberals or conservatives. Political Independency may, in fact, be a reflection of alienation or disengagement from the political system, not unlike the disengagement from the religious system.

There is no statistically significant correlation (Table 5.5) between "feminism" and church attendance for any of the conservatives or for the Independent or Republican moderates, and the correlations are weakest for liberal and moderate Democrats and strongest for Independent and Republican liberals. These latter two groups, incidentally, might be said to lack a supportive party base since the liberal Independent belongs to no party body and a liberal Republican belongs to a party which is very suspicious of liberals. The strongest negative correlations between "feminism" and church attendance seem to be found among those political groups which are most likely to be alienated. The political group for which ideological consistency might be most readily found—liberal Democrats—reveals only a moderate negative relationship between "feminism" and church attendance.

One might tentatively conclude that the angry "feminists" tend to be not so much ideologues as alienates and that perhaps church leadership responsive to the ideologues (however necessary and appropriate it may be) might achieve little effect on the alienates.

CHAPTER VII: ALIENATION, SUBCULTURE AND SEX

The angry Catholic "feminists" are those who do not have a great deal of confidence in church leadership. One might well wonder whether such alienation from church leadership applies merely to the church or to other social institutions also. In the Knights of Columbus Study of Young Adults, the respondents were asked about their confidence in other organizations--banks, major companies, education, executive branch of the government, organized labor, supreme court, judicial system. The responses to these questions were factor analyzed. One of the two factors that emerged loaded on banks, business companies, religion, and education.

The analysis described in Chapters I to III was repeated, using this alienation factor instead of attitude towards people running organized religion. The results, as summarized in Figure 6.1, were almost exactly the same. If one imagines the table as an inverted tree, each new level of branch represents a new variable added to the analysis. One can observe that only one branch on each limb represents a statistically significant relationship between church attendance and "feminism." There are five sets of branches: college attendance, alienation, working mother, mother's religious devotion, and closeness to God. On each level only one limb represents a statistically significant "fruit," each at a higher level of specification of the relationship. The statistically significant anger, in other words, is to be found only among those women respondents who went to college, were alienated from various social institutions, whose mothers did not work, whose mothers attended Mass once a week and who themselves do not feel very close to God.

Of the 32 branches on the top of the tree, one bears fruit. Of the 62 branches of the tree, only five depict statistical significance. On all other branches, there is no significant relationship between "feminism" and church attendance. Dissatisfaction with the church, then, seems to be a conduit through which conflicting images, past and present, affect a "feminist's" propensity to attend Mass frequently. But this dissatisfaction includes other major social institutions as well, probably because banks and financial institutions and educational institutions are also seen as responsible for the image of Woman one has inherited from one's mother.

The Knights of Columbus Study included Canada as well as the United States, making possible an analysis of four ethnic subcultures: English-Canadian, Anglo-American, French-Canadian and Hispanic-American. The English-Canadian women are the most likely to be "feminists" followed by the English-Canadian men and Anglo-American women. The other five groups -- Anglo-American men, French-Canadian men and women, Hispanic-American men and women -- differ greatly among themselves, although only among the Hispanics are the young adult men more likely (though not significantly) to be "feminists" than women (Table 6.2).

Statistically significant relationships between "feminism" and church attendance exist in half the groups -- French-Canadian and Anglo-American men, English-Canadian and Anglo-American women -- with the biggest difference being the 27 percentage point difference in church attendance for the English-Canadians (Table 6.3). When the model used to explain the difference between "feminists" and not "feminists" for American women was applied to English-Canadian women and French-Canadian men, it reduced the difference of 27 percentage points to statistical insignificance for the English-Canadian women though it had no effect on French-Canadian men, suggesting that English-Canadian women share with their American sisters the image incompatabilities we have already discussed whereas the dynamics at work among French-Canadian men seem to be quite different.

Despite the fact that American young men between the ages of eighteen and thirty are somewhat less likely to display a negative correlation between "feminism" and church attendance than their women counterparts, they are influenced by the same set of image incompatibilities as illustrated by Table 6.5 and 6.6. Significant relationship exists precisely and only between "feminists" and not "feminists" who attended college and precisely and only between college-educated "feminist" men whose mothers did not work when they were under six years old. Moreover, although the tables are not displayed, further specification parallel to that in the women's model occurs when mother's church attendance and sense of closeness to God are added to young American men.

The image incompatibility between the past and the present for young Catholic men is of the same sort as is to be found among young Catholic women. Although the differences between the "feminists" and the not "feminists" in church attendance are not quite as great for young American men as they are for young American women, the dynamics seem to be the same and represent a reaction against a childhood image of Woman/Church which is incompatible for "feminists"—male or female—with present image of Woman.

If approximately 350,000 young adult Catholic women are not going to Church because they see the Church identified with the old and traditional gender roles, almost 200,0000 young men are also not going to Church regularly because they do not accept strict gender roles which they see the Church as enforcing on the basis of their young men's childhood image of Church/Woman. The combination of those two images may indeed be unjustified. We have noted that our "feminists" in goodly numbers, both male and female, do not see the Church, either past or present, as identified with the traditional gender roles, at least not to such an extent that they withdraw from active church attendance (precisely, let it be repeated, because they experienced no such incompatibility in their childhood). Nonetheless, there are almost 600,000 young adults who are not going to Mass regularly because their image of Church identified with the gender role restrictions of the past (embodied in the past image of Woman) is perceived as incompatible with their present image of Woman.

It will not be sufficient for church leadership to respond by saying that these young people must amend their past image of Church to match the image of Church of many of their contemporaries who do not experience the Church versus Woman image incompatability of the present. One does not readily give up, even if one wants to, the experiences, the images and the stories which encode one's childhood experience of religion and sex roles. It is to the experiences, images and stories of the past that the Church must respond if it is to deal effectively with present alienation. Church leadership must assume responsibility, if not for the image of the past (an image, by the way, that many church leaders still promote today), at least for the present results of past images and experiences and stories.

CHAPTER VIII: "FEMINISM" AND MARRIAGE

William McCready has argued that there are two religious socialization experiences, childhood and marriage--the latter being a "second chance" for religion. In terms of the religious imagination
theory, the marriage experience is so powerful and so important in a
person's life that religious images and the religious story can be
modified both by the relationship with the spouse and by the spouse's
own religious images.

Thus, we wonder how the experience of marriage might affect the
complex network of image conflicts which seems to account for the lower levels of devotion among Catholic "feminists."

In the 1979 study of young adults, questionnaires were adminis-
tered to the spouses of respondents in the sample, and thus there is
an opportunity to investigate the impact of marriage on the religious
behavior of Catholic "feminists."

There is, first of all, a modest correlation of .18 between a
wife's score on the "feminism" scale and her husband's, about the
same as that between husband's and wife's religious imagination.
However, while the correlation between imaginations increases with
years of marriage, the correlation between "feminism" scores decreases. An analysis which compares duration of marriage with age in
their impact on this correlation led to the conclusion that age is
the important influence: among younger wives (under 25) there is a
much higher correlation with husband's "feminism" score (table 7.1)
--.33. Among wives over 25 the correlation decreases to an insignificant .07.

And this age effect is not a matter of there being more "feminist" young men available for the younger wives. The younger women (Table 7.2) "choose" husbands with similar attitudes on the role of women at a rate of more than half again as much as there are such men available in the population of husbands.

The word "choose" is used loosely because the consensus may have come as part of the general struggle for value compatibility which goes on both before and after a marriage begins. The husbands of these younger wives may have been "feminists" to begin with and hence were more attractive partners to their future wives, or they may have been "converted" as part of the courtship and early marriage value socialization. Or, finally, they may have been the "feminists" and may have converted their wives.

There are no effects of a wife's "feminism" on either the marital satisfaction or the sexual fulfillment of the wife. However, both indicators of marital adjust are affected by the husband's "feminism." Young women are more likely to be happily adjusted in their marriage if their husbands have a "modern" view on the role of women—regardless of what the woman's own perspective on women's roles might be. Perhaps a "feminist" husband is more sensitive to the needs and problems of his wife (Tables 7.3 and 7.4).

Both husband's and wife's "feminism" have a statistically significant impact on the sexual fulfillment of wives under 25 (tables 7.5 and 7.6) though only a wife's "feminism" affects the marital satisfaction of women who are older than 25. The higher level of value consensus in the marriages of young wives seems to be related to the importance of the impact on marriage of attitudes towards the role of women.

Thus, despite what one might have expected about the strains "feminism" might put on family life, the fact is that for young people it is not a liability but an asset to a happy marriage.

What effect does marriage have, then, on the devotion of a young Catholic woman who is a feminist?

"Feminists" are less likely to marry devout men—29% of their husbands attend church regularly as opposed to 39% of the husbands of not "feminists" (Table 7.8). However, the devotion of the husband has an overwhelming impact on the devotion of the "feminist" wife. Three quarters of the young "feminist" wives go to church regularly if their husband is also a regular attender—as opposed to two-thirds of the not "feminist" wives married to regularly attending husbands.

The devotion of the husband, then, seems to blot out the effect of "feminism" on church attendance (though the husband's devotion may be influenced by his wife's devotion). The husband is a religious influence so important that past image conflicts seem to become irrelevant.

Moreover, it would appear that devout husbands are especially likely to be "chosen" by those young "feminist" women who come from traditional families and whose "feminism" might have been expected to have the strongest negative effect on their religious devotion (Table 7.9) There is no difference in the church attendance of the husbands of "feminists" and the husbands of not "feminists," if the wife's mother worked before she was six but a 20 percentage point difference among those "feminists" whose mothers did not work.

Moreover, it is precisely among women under 25 that "feminists" are especially likely to be married to a husband who is devout, twice as likely in fact as their not "feminist" counterparts, while the reverse is true for those who are over 25, a group in which the not "feminists" are significantly more likely to choose a devout spouse (Table 7.10).

It would almost appear that such young women are seeking a husband whose religious devotion will cancel the negative relationship between images of Church and Woman from their childhood.

Do husbands influence wives or wives influence husbands in the search for family value consensus? McCready's intricate analysis of this "second chance" in religious socialization seems to suggest that husbands are more likely to be influenced by their wives than vice versa. However, our young "feminist" wives are aware of their husband's influence on their church attendance. It is among those women who perceive their husband as a "very great" influence on their religion (Table 7.11) that the difference between "feminists" and not "feminists" in religious devotion are eliminated, whereas the difference remains statistically significant among those women whose perception is that their husbands do not have a "very great" influence on their religion.

By way of contrast (Table 7.12), a perception that one's mother has a strong religious influence does not cancel out the negative impact of "feminism" on church attendance. Even though the wife may have had an effect on her husband's devotion, "feminist" young women seem to be aware that their husbands have had a strong impact on

55

them, one which has nullified to a very considerable extent their "anger" at the Church.

We pointed out earlier that non-traditional families seemed to open up to young women the possibility of being influenced by the non-traditional image of God as "Lover." It also is true (Table 7.13) that a combination of "feminist" wife and "feminist" husband notably increases the likelihood that a young woman will be extremely likely to think of God as a "Lover" (an image which, for all its seeming radicalism in a Jansenist and Puritanical Christianity, is at the core of the Christian and Jewish religious traditions, indeed the most important image of both traditions).

When a woman who rejects the traditional gender definitions joins forces in marriage with a husband who rejects them too, not only does the Church seem to obtain a better image, so, too, does God. From the point of view of the Catholic tradition, a marriage between two such young people is a highly desirable event.

If the image of Church as reflected by a devout husband is added to our path analytic flow chart, (Figures 7.1 to 7.4) we can observe a number of interesting phenomena in the differences between the dynamics affecting church attendance for "feminists" and non "feminists:"

1) The influence of the image of God as "Lover" in both models affects church attendance of a woman through the church attendance of her husband. The God image, it would appear is filtered through the husband image.

2) In both cases, it is the respondents whose mothers worked before they were six years old who are more likely to be married to a

devout husband, a phenomenon which is understandable for the "feminists," perhaps, since they are not caught up in the old tradition and hence may be looking for a new tradition to reinforce their religion, but less easily explained for the not "feminists."

3) Among the "feminists," there is a negative correlation between mother's church attendance and spouse's; those "feminists" who come from devout families may not want devout husbands because they see devotion as a component of traditional role models for women. On the other hand those feminists who come from non-traditional families are more likely to be married to devout husbands, perhaps because they are free to establish their own religious tradition. In terms of response to "feminism," the Church has a distinct advantage among those women whose background involves either a non devout or a working mother.

4) On the other hand, among the not "feminists" there is the expected correlation between mother's church attendance and spouse's church attendance. Religious socialization has the expected effect except when a modern image of Woman intervenes. This image reverses the expected effect.

5) A working mother has a direct and positive impact on the church attendance of her daughter, through the fact that she worked and not mediated by either her own devotion or that of her son-in-law but only if her daughter is a "feminist."

6) Because of the stronger influence of Church as reflected by husband, of the God image and of the non-traditional mother, the model for "feminists" explains twice as much of the variance in church attendance as does the model for not "feminists'." The balance and com-

plexity of the image system is more important for those caught in image conflicts.

7) By way of summary, a devout spouse and a non-traditional mother—both independently and together—play very important roles in determining whether or not "feminism" leads to anger and alienation from the Church.

The last two graphs (Figure 7.3 and 7.4) show that consciousness of spouse's influence is almost always mediated through spouse's actual church attendance and that the impact of both variables is much greater for "feminist" women. The model for them explains almost three-fifths of the variance in their church devotion while the model for not "feminist" women explains less than three-tenths of the variance. The correlation between husbands and wives is greater for "feminists" than for not "feminists" and the impact of consciousness of husband's influence is also greater for these women, suggesting that the correlation does is in fact represent a flow of influence from husband to wife.

When both husband and wife are "feminists," the variance explained is the same, but there is a direct relationship between husband's influence and wife's church attendance, indicating perhaps that if a "feminist" woman's husband is also a "feminist," he has an impact on her beyond the power of example leading to imitation.

"Feminism," in conclusion, is, if anything, a positive asset to a young marriage and a "feminist" husband has a direct impact on both his wife's image of God as a "Lover" and on her church attendance. The strength of the latter is in part the result of the propensity of a "feminist" woman from a non-traditional background to be more likely to choose a devout husband.

A woman's image of both God and Church, then, are affected by her experience with her husband and by the story of their relationship with one another. Such experiences are especially important for a "feminist" woman whose husband, particularly if he is devout and particularly if he is also a feminist, is able to be a strongly positive sacrament of both God and Church.

CHAPTER IX: THE INFLUENCE OF PRIESTS ON "FEMINISTS"

We have established in previous chapters that the "anger" of Catholic "feminists" is rooted in their past experience of Church as opposed to their present image of Woman. Apparently this image conflict is mitigated by marriage to a devout husband. Is there anything else the Church can do to correct its image problem with those who see the Church as supporting the traditional gender role of women? Can the institution in its ordinary pastoral work expect to undo the conflicts of the past? In particular, can priests make a contribution to the re-establishment of image harmony?

We intend to suggest in this chapter that there is some evidence for the tentative conclusion that the sympathetic parish priest can play a role in diminishing the "anger" of the "alienated" Catholic "feminist." Unfortunately, only a minority of priests seem qualified for such pastoral intervention.

There is little difference between the "feminists" and the not "feminists" in the proportion who feel that their parish priests are "very understanding" of human problems, the percentage who have had a serious talk with a priest in the past year and the proportion who say that a priest has had an important impact on their religious lives. Indeed, one-sixth of Catholic young women under 30 respond positively to the last two questions and only one-third to the first questions. Many young women (about one-third) are unable to rate the understanding of their parish priests because they do not have the information to make a judgment. However, among those who are able to judge, the "sympathy" of the parish priests is very important indeed for the "feminists" who, if they rate their parish priest as "very understanding," are as likely to go to Church as are those who are not "feminist." If the young woman has any information about her local clergyman, then her evaluation of his human sympathy is likely to be a very important counter to the negative effect of her "feminist" attitudes on her church attendance (Table 8.2).

Similarly, those "feminists" who say that a priest has influenced them greatly and who have had a serious conversation with a priest in the last year (Table 8.3) are as likely as their not "feminist" counterparts to attend church regularly (about three-fourths of both go to Mass almost every week).

And the image of God as a "Lover" correlates more strongly with the "understanding" of the parish priests and with the influence of a "priest" on the person's religious life for "feminists" than it does for not "feminists." In both the former cases, the correlation is statistically "significant," while in neither of the latter is it "significant." The priest seems to play a role similar to that of the devout husband and the non-traditional mother in opening the mind of a young woman to this image of God (Table 8.4). Both the sensitivity of the priest and the intensity of the image of God make their own contribution to the propensity of "feminist" women to go to Church, though the image of God seems to be more important in equalizing the church attendance rates of the "feminist" and the not "feminist." Thus, to a considerable extent, the priest's effectiveness seems to be mediated through the image of God which is associated with a woman's evaluation of his skills. It may be that the effective parish counselor does indeed act as a "sacrament"--a revelation--of an image of God which diminishes the inconsistency a woman might perceive between her image of the Church and her image of Woman (Table 8.5).

Similarly (Table 8.6) the influence of a priest on a woman's life seems to work through the image of God as a "Lover" to eliminate the difference in church attendance between "feminists" and not "feminists." We are dealing with very small numbers of respondents in this analysis, so we cannot speak with great confidence, but it is certainly possible to say that the importance of a priest in mediating a different image of God which cancels the inconsistency a woman perceives between her image of Church and of Woman cannot be rejected.

In addition to the small number of respondents available for this analysis, there is also the problem that it may well be that the women who are already well disposed towards the Church are those who give the clergy high ratings on influence and on counselling skills. That there is some relationship between evaluation of a priest's skill and actual contact with him can be judged, however, from Table 8.7. Both "feminists" and not "feminists" are more likely to rate their parish clergy as "very understanding" if they have had a talk with them in the last year than if they have not had such a talk; in the case of the former, the conversation makes for a statistically significant difference of 20 percentage points in the proportion saying that the priests are "very understanding" (Table 8.7).

But may it not be the fact that these "feminists" were devout women to begin with which led them to consult their clergy? Could it not be the case that in fact the priest has little effect on a woman's devotion and that rather the devotion causes her to consult the priest and to rate him highly, whether she is a "feminist" or not?

In the absence of an elaborate research design which would enable us to study women both before and after their contact with the clergy, we must rely for an answer to this question on a questionnaire item which asked the respondent to locate herself in a series of five concentric circles indicating her closeness to the church (and to God and to her parish) at the present time and also five years before the survey. By subtracting the present score from the past, we are able to obtain the respondent's evaluation of whether she is closer to the church now than she was five years ago.

Obviously a conversation with a priest (Table 8.8) does relate to a greater propensity to have "returned" to the church, significantly so for "feminists." Again there is a difference of 20 percentage points in the proportion who are closer to the Church between those "feminists" who have talked to a priest and those who have not.

It still is possible, of course, that they were on their way back in and that they approached the priest as part of that return. Nonetheless, the Church could ill afford to assume that the priest does not play an important role in the process.

The fact of the parish priest being "very understanding" also (Table 8.9) has a significant effect for "feminist" women on their return to the church—a 24 percentage point difference in the proportion "returning" as opposed to a 5 percentage point difference for not "feminists"--whose return rates are lower because they are less likely to have been at a distance from the Church and have less ground to travel. Nonetheless both the conversation with the priest and the sympathy of the priest seems more important for the "feminists" than for the not "feminists," presumably because the former have more of a problem with church leadership than do the latter and are more responsive to a clergy who represent sensitive and sympathetic church leaders.

Finally, which is more important, the fact of conversing with a priest or your evaluation of the clergy's understanding of human problems (an evaluation which does not necessarily result from your conversation, though of course it probably is not uninfluenced by it)?

Clearly, a conversation without a high regard for the priest's empathy (Table 8.10) is not of much help to leading to a return of Catholic "feminists" (though it does seem to help the not "feminists"). Thus, while one cannot say with absolute certainly --both because of the small number of respondents involved and because of the intricate nature of the analysis--it does seem very likely that for "feminists" a return to the Church is greatly facilitated by a conversation with an understanding priest. And in the absence of the actual conversation, an awareness that there are understanding priests in one's parish is a notable help.

There is, then, no iron determinism in the childhood linkage between traditional Church and traditional Woman's roles. A devout husband and/or a sympathetic parish priest can help break such a linkage.

Nonetheless, most young women do not give their clergy high grades on their understanding of human problems and only one out of six has actually talked to a priest in the last year. When "fem-

64

inists" do seek out priests with whom to talk, they seem not unsatis-fied with the results of their conversations (though perhaps they also select priests whom they think will be sympathetic).

What kind of pastoral skills does a priest need to be able to fa-cilitate a woman's transitional experience as she tentatively consid-ers whether her "feminism" and her religion can after all be consistent?

The only answer to that question is that there is no sociological evidence available as to what the required skills might be. But church leaders might at least ponder the fact that two-thirds of Catholic young women do not think priests have these skills.

CHAPTER X: SOCIOLOGICAL CONCLUSION

The modestly popular play Sister Mary Ignatius Explains It All
is a devastating attack by a very angry playwright on the Catholic education and the Catholic church of his childhood. Sister Mary
Ignatius is an arrogant, rigid, narrow, oppressive manifestation of
counter reformation Catholicism. No one familiar with the Church of a
quarter century ago will deny the reality of such persons, even if
they were not the only kind of parochial school teachers in that era.

But one wonders why the fury at her and what she stood for, a fury which can be found in many other alienated Catholic writers. That
form of Catholicism is as dead as Arianism. By now Sister Mary
Ignatius is either married to a priest or marching on a picket line.
She is as rigid as she ever was, but Catholics have no monopoly on
rigidity.

Yet the angry writers and the other angry Catholics of that generation will not be put off by such a response. They don't care what
Catholicism is today. They are still angry at what it was and the relationship between what it was and the problems in their lives.
Indeed, they do not want to hear that the Church has changed, because
a change will have deprived them of a convenient scapegoat.

To say that the Church is a scapegoat for their anger is not to
justify the Catholicism of Sister Mary Ignatius or to criticize the
anger of those who still hate her and what she stood for. But not everyone who sat in classrooms presided over by such nuns is angry at
the Church. The issue then becomes why some Catholics focus on one aspect of the Catholic tradition and others on another aspect. The im-

66

age of Sister Mary Ignatius represents an intensely unpleasant experience in the playwright's childhood and the image lingers, affecting even today his image of Church. His experience of her has become a symbol which is an important part of his life story. Perhaps the story can be changed—our data suggest it might be by a devout and progressive and loving Catholic spouse—but it will not be changed easily.

Religious images, in this theory, are preconscious—not repressed but not attended to either. They become patterns, paradigms, templates for response to life and to religion as well as symbols of past experiences. The phenomenon which we have investigated in this monograph is but one of a whole species of religious reactions in which an institution is judged by a past experience, an experience which is intense, frustrating and infuriating but which was not the only possible experience even in the past.

Yet to those who suffered the experience, it seems to have been the only possible one until some new and powerful experience deletes it. Those who are bitterly angry at the Sister Mary Ignatius's of their past simply cannot believe that all Catholics do not share such an experience. Those "feminist" women who are "turned off" by the Church are doubtless astonished and sceptical when they encounter other "feminist" women whose experiences do not preclude high levels of religious devotion.

The key, of course, is the family. I had a couple of teachers not unlike Sister Mary Ignatius in school and laughed them off because my family experience was benign for the most part and what was not benign was not identified with the Church. Moreover, whatever conflicts I've had in adult life have not come from ambivalent family experiences which are linked in my imagination with Church.

As a psychiatrist once remarked, "I know a priest has begun to mature when he stops blaming his problems on the seminary and begins to examine his family experiences."

Again, these comments are made not to excuse the Church of the past or the Church of the present for their attitudes towards women, which I find deplorable and intolerable. Rather, they are an attempt at an explanation of why these attitudes drive some "feminist" women away from the Church and do not drive others away.

Briefly, there are four persons who seem to suppress the negative correlation between "feminism" and church attendance-- Mother, Spouse, Priest and God. The Mother must be non-traditional either in her church attendance or her occupational career. The Spouse must be devout and it helps if he is also a "feminist." And God must be seen as a "Lover," which She/He is likely to become if the Spouse and the Mother are appropriate "sacraments."

The point in these observations is that negative images and image incompatibilities are deep and complex but not utterly immutable. The family past probably cannot be changed or even reexamined, short of intense therapy. The Spouse is at least a new influence and a new image which is of enormous importance. Do you want to bring a "feminist" young woman back to Church? Well, find her a devout, loving, and "feminist" spouse. There is a chance that she is already looking for one anyway.

And if God does not change, surely the image the Church presents of Him/Her can change (change back, I would suggest). In part, perhaps, the personalities of Church leaders can help affect such a change. Pope John surely had such an impact, as did John Paul I, the smiling September Pope (who, in keeping with a little known but power-ful church tradition, talked of God as a Mother). So did John Paul II until his image took on a tone of nay saying and repression (an image I happen to think is inaccurate but which is almost universal, espe-cially among those who have a negative image of Church to begin with).

However, "let's get to know one another" sessions in the parish or the election of women to parish councils or the appointment of wo-men to diocesan "cabinets"--however meritorious such actions and ac-tivities may be--will simply not touch the image incompatibilities which this research has unearthed.

If church leaders are interested in actually "evangelizing" alienated Catholic women, instead of merely talking about it, then they must resign themselves to the fact that they have an enormous problem on their hands, a problem rooted in the mistakes of the past indeed but confirmed by continuing mistakes in the present.

And probably the first change ought to be in their own personal-ities and attitudes.

Alas, clergy (of all faiths) are much better at telling others to change than at changing themselves.

And now to my theological sibling who can speak with much better authority than I can about the insensitive chauvinism of clerics, past and present.

THEOLOGICAL REFLECTION

by Mary G. Durkin

CHAPTER XI: A THEOLOGY OF SEXUALITY

At some time in human history individual persons, and eventually groups of persons, began to reflect on the significance of sexual differentiation. We have no record of this initial reflection, but from our perspective it seems safe to say that at some point humans began to wonder "Why?—Why masculinity? Why femininity?" The "why" might have been occasioned by the mystery of the obvious sexual differences—lactation, bleeding and the ability to bear children in women, facial hair and external sex organs in the man. Or perhaps the question was linked to the why of the emotional bond that developed between a man and a woman who parented an offspring. Whatever the occasion of the question when it was asked among earliest humans or when it is asked by their descendants in the present day, the answer which might seem to be a legitimate response to the question is never completely satisfying. There remains a continual quest for the deeper reasons for sexual differentiation and its pervasive influence in so many aspects of our life. It is this continual quest for understanding of sexuality and of its bodily and emotional manifestations that leads us to identify sexuality questions in their ultimate form as questions of mystery. How we answer these questions strongly reflects what we believe about the ultimate meaning of life. In some instances the answers we acquired in our youth were directly linked to our understanding of God in our religious tradition; in other instances the answers came through our perspective of life's ultimate meaning acquired somewhat unconsciously in family experiences in our earliest years. Sex and the body are good or sex and the body are bad, and men do this and women do that and parenthood is good or parenthood is a drag are ideas initially conveyed in family experience and reinforced or questioned by larger social communities, particularly by our religious community.

The link between the "feminist's" anger at the Church and her perception of woman's role acquired from her mother and at variance with her present understanding of women calls for an evaluation of the Church's contribution to a negative image of Woman. But before addressing this topic and offering suggestions for positive improvement, it is necessary to consider the whole issue of a religious understanding of sexuality. The difficulty of the Church witnessing to a positive image of women in the contemporary world is rooted in the Church's lack of a positive theology of sexuality. Both the awe and the fear, which are part of the mystery of human sexuality, require a transformation by our faith if we are to encourage Christians to discover the giftedness of sexual diversity. The fear of a movement toward sexual equality is deeply rooted and will not easily disappear. Even the best-intentioned Christians will have difficulty eradicating sexist behavior without an appreciation of how this behavior is contrary to the Christian vision of human sexuality.

A theology of sexuality, which acknowledges the power of the human sexual drive and the influence this drive has for behaviors in all areas of human relationships, would have much to offer to Christian women wanting to respond positively to a cultural situation vastly different than that of previous generations of women. In this chapter we will examine the mysterious dimensions of human sexuality and consider why we need to develop a theology of sexuality which will encourage people to maximize the positive potential of sexuality and minimize its demonic possibilities.

Pope John Paul II in his audience addresses on a theology of sexuality refers to the creation of masculinity and femininity as a basic fact of human existence that has had profound implications for every era of human history[1]. Each new era must evaluate, in the Pope's words must "discern and judge," its own experience of sexuality in light of the ultimate meaning of life revealed in its faith tradition. Unfortunately, organized religion has often limited its discussion of sexuality-related issues to a consideration of concerns of community survival, since for most of human history the survival of the community depended upon strict control of its reproductive capabilities. A religious rationale for this control—rules for specific sex roles and sexual behaviors tied into the ultimate meaning of life proclaimed by a religion—was a strong support for the social emphasis on survival. The contemporary situation, with its increased lifespan and decreased infant mortality rate, has lessened the social emphasis on reproductive survival and to a certain degree, increased the possibility of encountering Mystery in reflection on human sexuality. The rules approach had regulated thinking about sexuality to a point where the question of "why male and female?" was answered only by reference to reproduction; to a certain degree, rules robbed even that reproductive aspect of some of its mysterious dimension. Now, perhaps more than at any other time in human history, we are challenged to reflect upon the bonding aspect of the human sexual attraction and its implications for human relationships.

Scholars who have studied the evolution of <u>home sapiens</u> from earlier hominid cultures have hypothesized that the genetic root of <u>human</u> sexuality extends back into our hominid beginnings. The survival of our particular species is attributed to the fact that the unique quasi pair-bonding of <u>homo sapiens</u>, which bound a man to the mother of his children, allowed the offspring to develop the skills necessary for survival in a hunting and gathering culture. Investigations of primitive cultures and of archeological remains of early prehistoric cultures led to the hypotheses that the bonding necessary for the survival of the clan or the tribe had an emotional component, aspects of which were realized even though cultural development tended to emphasize reproduction to the exclusion of emotional bonding. Powerful sexual attraction between the human male and human female assured the survival of <u>homo sapiens</u> in our earliest beginnings. Regulation of that sexual attraction in the various cultural settings developed by different groups of humans assured the continual survival of a variety of cultures. Now that we are more aware of the bonding possibilities of human sexuality and less compulsive about our reproductive needs, we are in a position where we can put aside sexual stereotypes and rules and regulations valid for the needs of previous cultures and examine more carefully the pervasiveness of sexuality for the individual and the society as a whole.

The old saying, "The more I know, the more I know I don't know," captures the feeling of mystery we experience when we reflect on all of the understandings of human sexuality discovered through the scientific study in our contemporary world. Both at a scientific and a popular level we understand much more about the physical and psychological aspects of human sexuality. Still, as we reflect on our own personal experience and on the experiences of other humans, we realize there is tremendous confusion over how to maximize the positive potential of human sexuality,. We sense a need to "control" the pervasiveness of this aspect of the human personality; we search in vain for the scientific understanding that will help us control our erotic tendencies and rid ourselves of our sexist inclinations, help us be comfortable with our bodies, allow us to embrace new family roles and assist us as we educate our young in an appreciation of sexuality. We are able to admit to the positive possibilities of human sexuality, but we also have ample evidence of its demonic potential.

We in the modern world, oftentimes unconsciously, are searching for a key to an integrated approach to growth and development in the sexuality aspects of our personality. We want to be at ease with our bodies and capable of intimacy that is neither self nor other-destructive. We want to enjoy the pleasurable aspects of sexuality and we want the emotional comfort of a commitment of intimacy. The more we search for this integrated approach to sexuality, the more we are confronted with awesomeness and terror. The more we recognize the mystery of human sexuality, the more we sense the need to relate our search for understanding of sexuality to our search for the ultimate meaning of life. We need a religious perspective that will challenge us to aim for this integrated approach.

The contemporary theologian asked to articulate how the Catholic tradition might contribute to this modern search for an integrated sexual identity must overcome some obstacles from previous centuries of Judeo-Christian reflection on sexuality. A realization that particular cultural needs required an emphasis on reproduction and indirectly contributed to a condemnation of the demonic possibilities of sexuality with little celebration of its positive potential makes the contemporary theologian leery of a theology rooted only in the experience of a particular culture. However, the need of the modern culture for an integrated vision of human sexuality seems to require that the theologian examine how the beliefs of our faith tradition relate to the basic fact of bodily sexuality and its implications for human personhood.

Our approach to developing a positive theology of sexuality for the contemporary world begins not with an analysis of previous Church statements on the specific issue of sexuality, but with a consideration of the basic doctrines of our Catholic Christian tradition. This should help us as we seek to appreciate the sacramental possibilities of the Mystery we encounter when we experience the extraordinary possibilities of our sexuality. Pope John Paul II in a series of weekly audience addresses on a theology of sexuality and the body offers one model for how we might develop a religious response to the contemporary experience of sexuality.

Though the Pope's analysis is philosophical and abstract, his poetic imagination leads him to uncover in certain scriptural passages new levels of meaning which help us see how the doctrines of Creation, Incarnation, Grace, Redemption and the Holy Spirit can be applied to the contemporary experience of sexuality in a transformative way. The Pope appears to correlate with these doctrines the scientific findings regarding sexuality as bonding for human relationships. His theology of sexuality could be considered a theology of bonding.

In an examination of Christ's response to the Pharisee's question on divorce, the Pope sees Jesus' reference to "the beginning" as a direction to uncover the Divine Plan for human sexuality in the Genesis creation story. This plan becomes our criteria for judging a correct response to sexuality in every time and every place. The creation story in Genesis I and II reveals that God created humankind, male and female, in "the image of God" so that through the unity of "two in one flesh" a man and a woman might model Divine Love; through their unselfish gift of themselves to each other, they would demonstrate how love of the unique and unrepeatable personhood of the other must be at the root of all relationships. The Genesis story reveals that Divine Love enters the world only through the human body and sexuality, emphasizing the sacramental nature of the body and of masculinity and femininity.

The first man alone and the first woman alone could not image God, but in the joining of their exterior and interior differences they brought a completeness to humanity which allowed them to be "in the image of God." Their bodies and their sexuality were given to them by God as a gift (a grace) so that they might reflect Divine Love, so they might be lovers as God is a Lover. They participate even more fully in this grace when, as the story of the birth of the first human in Genesis IV indicates, "with the help of the Lord" a new creature springs forth from their bodily union. The bonding potential of sexuality must be responded to for "the help of the Lord" to be present in procreation.

By emphasizing the sacramental nature of the body and of sexuality, a pastoral theology true to the doctrine of Creation could use this Papal interpretation of Genesis as a basis for helping people transform their experience of sexuality. When people reflect upon the bonding possibilities offered by the powerful sexual attraction of man for woman and woman for man, this theology encourages them to use their sexual attraction in a positive way so as to reflect the God in whose image they are created.

Our bodies and our sexuality, as part of Divine creation, were looked upon by God and judged to be "good." The doctrine of Creation, understood more fully through this interpretation, sees the body and sexual union as challenges to men and women to enter into relationships in which each respects the personhood of the other who is an "other self."

Unfortunately, as the Pope's analysis of Genesis III indicates, God's plan for male/female relationships suffered when the first human opted for "the things of the world" in the tree of knowledge of good and evil as opposed to "the things of God," changing the male/female relationship from a relationship of gift to a relationship of appropriation.

As a result of this original loss of appreciation of the bonding potential of sexuality, humans become prey to the three forms of lust mentioned in I John, leading to a shame of the body and of sexuality which really marks their greater shame at their choice for "things of the world." Still humans are not condemned to never experience the sacramental value of their body. Christ's words to the Pharisees are issued in the context of his promise of redemption, a liberation that includes the redemption of the body. His direction to reconsider God's plan in Genesis is issued with the understanding that the possibility of fulfilling this plan is offered again in the gift (grace) of redemption.

The paradoxical nature of Christ's teachings which challenges his followers to transform their experiences of sexuality is evident, according to the Pope's analysis, in Christ's words in the Sermon on the Mount regarding "adultery in the heart." The emphasis which the Jewish religious tradition had placed on adultery in the body lent religious support to the cultural tradition of male/female sex roles and saw adultery as a sin possible only when a man and a woman who were not married to each other, joined so as to become "one flesh." But if adultery is looked upon as the lust which chooses the "things of the world" rather than the "things of God," then Christ's words concerning adultery in the heart are a condemnation of any activity which fails to recognize the Divine Plan for our bodies to be the means for persons to be gift to each other. Adultery in the heart occurs when the other person in a relationship is viewed as an object for one's sexual satisfaction rather than a person with whom one could join in such a way as to reflect God, even if that person is one's spouse.

The need for a pastoral application of this theological interpretation of the redemption of the body calls for a deeper examination of how people in our contemporary culture search for a transformation of their experiences of sexuality. We must address these issues from a perspective that sees the body and sexuality as good, as sacramental, but as in need of the grace of redemption, recognizing that, at times, we allow our bodies to lead us to choose the "things of the world" rather than the "things of God." The promise of the grace of redemption as a help to deepen our appreciation of the sacramental capability of sexuality needs to be included in any discussion of how Christ's redemption speaks to our contemporary situation.

The Pope sees Christ's call to be "pure in heart" as a call to choose the "things of God" rather than the "things of the world." Though this call refers to purity in the generic sense and not specifically to bodily sexual purity, the Pope finds bodily sexual purity included in the general call to be "pure in heart." His analysis of the Pauline doctrine of the Holy Spirit stresses purity of heart, which is both a gift given by the Spirit and a virtue which we must cultivate. This purity of heart as the opposite of adultery in the heart comes through our recognition of our bodies as temples of the Holy Spirit, as sacraments which allow us to reveal Divine Love. We must learn to celebrate the bonding potential of our sexuality.

The Papal theology of sexuality and the body, with its promise of continuing help from the Holy Spirit to the human search for understanding of sexuality, supplies a perspective in which to address the awe and the terror of the contemporary experience of sexuality. The pastoral theologian, listening to the questions raised by the experience of sexuality in the modern world, finds in the Papal addresses a framework for relating our faith traditions to this most basic of human experiences. We find the key to an integrated approach to growth and development in the sexuality aspects of personality in an appreciation of the bonding of "two in one flesh" possible when each person respects the personhood of the other; together they are "in the image of God," reflecting the love of God.

The Papal theology challenges both the previous negative attitudes of church teachings on sexuality and the present almost "obsessive," critical reaction of some religious leaders to contemporary interest in sexuality. Many previous church statements ignored the bonding possibilities of sexuality celebrated in his poetical interpretation of scriptural passages. Modern concerns about sexuality would seem, in the Pope's analysis, to be worthy of our attention since contemporary religious thought has failed to pay enough attention to the revelatory possibilities of sexuality. The underlying message of his talks seems to be: sexuality and the body are good because they were created by God, redeemed by Christ and are continually graced by the presence of the Holy Spirit. The redemption of the body "liberates" us because it frees us to appreciate the bonding of our sexual attraction as a respect for the personhood of the "other self." In the next chapter we will consider how a pastoral theology of femininity flows quite naturally from this theology of sexuality. We will seek to show how the experience of woman's quest for identity in the modern world, when transformed by a positive theology of sexuality, offers a religious support for women in the contemporary world.

Angry Catholic women have an image of the Church as an institution which does not recognize their personhood. A development of this theology of sexuality, which emphasizes the personhood of women, might not resolve the negative image of the Church experienced by an alienated "feminist." Still, church leaders, theologians and pastoral workers, who are committed to translating this theology into images and stories which would speak to people's experiences could possibly spark a positive religious experience for an angry Catholic woman, especially if these professional church persons are willing to search for and apply the implications of this theology in their personal lives and their professional endeavors.

CHAPTER XII: A CELEBRATION OF FEMININITY

Probably for the first time in human history women are free from the constraints of societal reproductive demands. The possible responses to this freedom confront women with new choices. At the same time women are losing support for living according to old stereotypes.

The young woman at the supermarket checkout counter telling her friend about the previous evening's "bachelorette" party at a male strip parlor is but one example of the complexity of issues facing women in the modern world. Should women disparage their past contributions to human life and seek to emulate men's way of being human (becoming "bachelorettes" and going to strip shows are perhaps frivolous examples but they are modeled after male behavior)? Or should women be reflective about their skills and talents, uncovering ways in which their past experiences give them insights into how to apply these skills and talents in new situations? Will the result of the present cultural revolution be a male-modeled society or will the feminine dimension of human experience, cultivated in the past by women, lead to a new model of human behavior which integrates both the masculine and the feminine dimension of human personhood? The sociological investigation of angry Catholic women indicates that for these women the struggle to find an answer to questions about feminine identity in the modern world is complicated by the image they have of the Church as a supporter of traditional role models. For these women this support leads to their alienation from the institutional Church. The church community which supported their mothers in the practices of traditional behavior is not seen as supportive of modern woman's search for new behavior patterns. Church leaders, hoping to counter this negative image of the Church, must root their response to this highly crucial issue in an appreciation of how a theology of the body and of sexuality clarifies the ambiguity most Christians experience when confronted with the reality of changing sex roles.

A brief review of the development of role stereotypes will provide some hints concerning the dilemma women face as they seek to establish their identity in today's world and will set the stage for our theological reflection. When cultural and religious concerns regarding the powerful human sexual attraction were limited to the need for reproductive growth, stereotypes of male and female behavior were inevitable. Though specific gender-related tasks differed from one culture to another, in every culture some gender differences existed and were related to community survival. Explanations for why men and women would sublimate their power sexual attraction to the needs of the larger society were found in the "will of the gods." The inevitable mystery experienced in the encounter with another human being like you yet unlike you, necessary for the continuation of the community and, in many instances, emotionally important to you, was explained in terms of a Divine Plan and in some instances as a failure of or a sin against that plan. Rules and rituals regarding sex, fertility, and male and female roles assured continued favor with the gods, with the result that gender-related behavior, the root of many of today's stereotypes, was deeply ingrained in religious traditions and rarely subjected to questioning. As a consequence, sexuality was robbed of much of its mystery. For many people the lack of attention to emotional bonding meant no emphasis on both the awe and the terror-filled possibilities of sexuality. Sexuality was just one more of the drudgeries of human existence. Much of the sexual symbolism of religious practices was lost as sex came to be considered a less sacred aspect of life.

The process of stereotyping male and female behavior deprived women and men of their ability to regard each other as a source of mystery, a source of God's presence to each other and to the world. They could not appreciate their own sexuality as a source of Divine Revelation. Women, who bore babies and bled regularly in a mysterious way which caused men to experience wonder and terror, never appreciated their mystery because purification rituals turned these revelatory possibilities into inferior types of human behavior less pleasing to God than the activities of men.

We do not know the exact steps which led to this cultural development, but a review of the Old Testament literature makes it apparent that at the time this literature was recorded Judaism was established as a patriarchal tradition which considered women inferior. There are a few references to the possibilities of a relationship where man and woman are equal persons and a sacrament of God—i.e., Genesis II and the Song of Songs;—but, for the most part, the Old Testament rules and rituals supported the societal need for women's dedication to reproduction and considered women's activities part of the profane area of human existence.

Jesus, according to some Scripture scholars, challenged the stereotypes of his day in his relationships with women.[1] The Church, developed in response to his demand to spread the Good News, did not appear to hear his call to transform the situation of women and to reestablish the Divine Plan which would allow a man and a woman to unite in one flesh and to be a sign of God's love. For church leaders and scholars the societal view of women won out over the transformative view of Jesus. Though women were influential in the Church through their roles in various religious orders, even a woman like Teresa of Avilla continually refers to herself as only a woman and, consequently, more susceptible to temptation.

The stereotypes, developed by a society and reinforced by its religious beliefs, applied to a society that no longer exists. Industrial and technological advances, accompanied as they were by a lower infant mortality rate and longer life span, relieved society of the need to be overly concerned about the reproductive behavior of its people. Still, many of the rules of both the society and the Church continue to be based on the past needs of society.

The story of woman's inferior status and of the tacit support church theology, rules and rituals gave to this view has been documented over and over in the work of feminist scholars. It is only with the advent of advanced education for women and reliable means of birth control, however, that a movement began to challenge the validity of these stereotypes and their implied evaluation of woman's potential for full personhood. Though there were earlier movements of women for "liberation," especially for suffrage, the circumstances of the 1960's and 70's were such that large numbers of women, even when not identifying with the Feminist cause, felt themselves caught up in identity crisis. Today the old stereotypes no longer seem valid for many women's experiences; but as they seek new models of behavior, they are confronted with the strong hold these stereotypes have on the individual and collective imagination of the society.

The angry Catholic "feminist" is not unlike many of her peers in her search for a viable identity. For the most part, women of the era of the 70's and the 80's grew up with a traditional image, indeed stereotype, of male and female roles. Confronted with the opportunity to move beyond these stereotypic roles, they have no strong image that would help them respond to this challenge, save for what they have witnessed in the behavior of men. In some instances they feel pressured to give up the stereotypic image of the traditional woman for the stereotypic image of the liberated woman who acts "just like a man." This new stereotype often requires giving up many of the traditional feminine activities which have been nurtured by women through the ages because these activities interfere with "success" according to a male standard.

A movement towards new stereotypes could decrease the confusion many women experience in their quest for feminine identity. But from the religious perspective, the new stereotypes, like the old stereotypes, will rob femininity of its mysterious power. The challenge of the 80's is to recognize the pluralism of women's experience and to develop an appreciation of how the positive aspects of human nature which have been guarded through the ages by the feminine experience can assist each woman as she makes decisions about her own identify.

There has not been an opportunity for women, except in a reactionary manner a la Maribel Morgan's <u>The Total Woman</u>, to be reflective about the positive aspects of human existence which they have cultivated during the long period of human history. Without this reflection and the ability to celebrate the positive contribution of the feminine dimension of human nature, women fail to acknowledge the importance of femininity. They tend to ignore the demonic potential of the male role model they seek to emulate. Or in some instances, the "superwoman" finds herself combining the demonic aspects of both male and female role stereotypes. Or the housewife will come to consider all aspects of previous female behavior as inferior and tend to identify herself as inferior. The 1980's are exciting times for women but they also demand a serious consideration of the contribution femininity has made to the growth and development of an understanding of human nature.

The theology of sexuality developed in the previous chapter, with its emphasis on unique and unrepeatable personhood of both the man and the woman, encourages us to investigate the contribution of femininity to the human ability to reflect the God in whose image we are created. The feminine experience is not second class human behavior, rather it is a manifestation of certain aspects of human nature which in turn reflect the God who created that nature. The redemption of the body made possible by Jesus Christ and continued through the presence of the Holy Spirit encourages us to reflect upon woman's experience and to recognize its importance for our understanding of how we, in this time and in this place, might better appreciate our body and our sexuality as a sacrament of Divine Love. The unity of man and woman called for in the original Divine Plan outlined in Genesis II reveals the homogeneity of man and woman and at the same time, celebrates the physical diversity which allows the man and woman to be "gift" to each other and thus to reflect most fully the Divine Image.

Today, perhaps for the first time in human history, we are increasingly aware of the homogeneity of man and woman as the lines are blurred between the world of work and the world of home. Men are assuming a greater proportion of the parenting roles; women are demonstrating their ability to be successful not only in white collar careers but also in jobs that require a physical strength and endurance previously thought lacking in women. This ability of both men and women to assume tasks generally limited to the other sex would seem to be a first step toward acknowledging the "equal" personhood of both men and women and could be a hopeful sign for those who would want to work toward the ideal of male/female relations contained in our theology of sexuality. But the reality of the situation seems to be that many of those tasks previously considered part of "woman's world" are being jettisoned because they are viewed as negative experiences forced upon women which neither a "free" woman nor a "feminist oriented" man would ever choose to do.

The theology of sexuality found in the analysis of Scripture in the previous chapter indicates that, even though throughout history, the male/female relationship has been primarily a relationship of appropriation rather than a relationship of gift, the human body and human sexuality retained hints of the original Divine Plan. The redemption offered by Jesus was the redemption of transformation, helping us to discover the basic goodness of human masculinity and femininity which had become clouded by our inability to hear God's original plan. The societal emphasis which limited our ability to recognize aspects of human sexuality other than reproductive led, at times, to an overemphasis on certain behaviors which tend to be demonic (for example, masochism in a man and overpowering motherhood in a woman). Still, in the division of labor that evolved in our Western society, certain positive aspects of human nature came to be emphasized as the "natural" province of women; a good part of the identity crisis many women experience today is attributable to their uncertainty about the validity of their past experiences at the same time that these experiences still exercise a powerful hold on their imagination and its image of femininity.

A pastoral theology of femininity rooted in our theology of sexuality should begin by investigating those areas of human nature which have been the "specialities" of women and by considering what insights into the meaning of human nature are to be found in the positive aspects of these feminine experiences. The aim of this exercise in pastoral theology is to help women discover how their faith perspective calls them to celebrate the positive potential of the feminine experience by bringing the richness of that experience to the choices they make in the new situations with which they are confronted in today's world.

As an example of how this process works, we will consider one of these specialities. We will examine the traditional role of the housewife, which is the subject of much debate at this period in womens experience. This particular speciality of women has gained negative connotations in discussions of women's past oppression and in considerations of an appropriate lifestyle for a modern woman. Following the example of Kathryn Allen Rabuzzi in her book The Sacred and the Feminine: Toward a Theology of Housework,[2] we will consider what it is in this activity that might be considered a manifestation of "humanness." A theology of sexuality would encourage a celebration of this humanness.

Our analysis of housework will be limited to how it was practiced by the traditional women who most probably influenced the imaginations of the angry Catholic women; since these women are a limited group of modern women, our pastoral theology is limited, but the insights into women's experience obtained in this analysis could be applicable to other groups of women who have similar basic images of femininity.

Rabuzzi argues that the feminine dismissal of housework as "shitwork" fails to realize the significance of housework in the life of the traditional woman. The same is true of the general attitude that looks upon most housework as degrading activity to be completed as quickly as possible in order to get on with the important things of life. She argues that if the home functions as sacred space, then the traditional housewife is the priestess who through the ritual enactment of housework turned an ordinary profane place into an extraordinary sacred space. A home is sacred space when family members "come home" to it for salvation. In such a home family members experience rootedness, sanctuary, containment, mystery and a centeredness which allowed them to be "at home" with themselves. According to Rabuzzi, the ability to be at home with ourselves

91

relates to the home's function as a symbol of both salvation and damnation and, hence, a symbol of ultimate concern. The traditional housewife/priestess, through her ritualistic housework, created the world of the home, which held things together so family members could orient themselves to the wider world and the universe. The mode of being of the housewife/priestess, as she engaged in her ritual tasks, was that of waiting, while the mode of being of those who function in the world beyond the home was that of questing.

The waiting mode of being with its repetitive housewifely tasks is often viewed as boring--how could anyone really enjoy dusting the same furniture every day for thirty years?--but Rabuzzi argues that traditional women's lives, like minimalist art, can lead to a mystical state through the manipulation of its "boring" aspects. Though many would look upon housework as meaningless and demonically boring, the traditional housewife/priestess, as she went about creating the "world" of her home, helped to transcend the chaos which occurs when people have no sense of centeredness and rootedness.

In her ordering of the sacred space of the home, the traditional housewife was the link between women of different generations. The skills of the traditional housewife are not acquired simply by following written directions. Any woman who has attempted to make a dress finds that even fairly explicit pattern directions do not make a seamstress. So, too, favorite family recipes that contain "a handful of this and a pinch of that" are seldom equaled in taste or appeal by "kitchen tested," professionally-designed recipes. The housekeeping of the traditional housewife/priestess was an art, one of the last "skills" to be "passed on" from one generation of family to the next.

Ironically, many of the tasks of traditional housework which were dismissed as irrelevant are applauded when men practice them in their careers or when women today perform them on a professional basis. For example, gourmet cooking and clothes designing as professional careers are rated as exciting and fulfilling, while the housewife who cooked and sewed is looked upon with a certain degree of pity. Today, even the housewife who is herself a gourmet cook or skilled seamstress or craft maker often feels pressure to abandon these tasks in favor of "more meaningful" activities in the real world beyond the home. The decline in sales of sewing machines and fabrics and the increase in sales of fast foods as the staple of American diets are an indication of the decreasing popularity of two aspects of the life of the traditional housewife/priestess.

A woman in her early fifties, who during her child-rearing years frequently entertained friends and her husband's business associates and was well-known for her gourmet cooking, recently applied her skills developed as a volunteer fund-raiser to a marketing career. She "no longer has the time" to entertain at home, so she and her husband take their guests to restaurants for dinner. On one of these outings, after a harried day of "questing," she realized that the Beef Wellington specialty of the well-known chef was not as tasty as the one she had often prepared for her guests. As she listened to the praise her fellow diners heaped upon the chef, she mentally compared the satisfaction she had experienced after a "successful" dinner party to her "success" as a marketing manager and briefly wondered if the latter success was worth sacrificing the satisfactions of the former.

Even though we might agree with Rabuzzi that the ritualistic enactment of the traditional housewife/priestess role creates an environment where family members can develop a sense of self-awareness and, therefore, that the task of housework does make a positive contribution, we still must wonder if the achievement of a feeling of "at homeness" for family members is worth sacrificing the talents of the women who functioned as housewife/priestess. What value did the housewife/priestess experience as she went about her ritualistic tasks? From a theological perspective, we ask if there was anything in the waiting mode of being that allowed humans to transcend the ordinariness of daily tasks and discover an insight into the ultimate meaning of human existence.

Also, in our modern technological society many women are in the work force, but few share in the excitement of the board room: for most working women, just as for most men the questing world appears to offer few hints about the way to salvation. We need to consider how the traditional housewife/priestess overcame the ordinariness of housework without succumbing to its demonic pull of boredom. Over and above the creation of a "place to come home to" for other family members, how did the traditional housewife/priestess, tied as she was to the rootedness of the home, achieve personal salvation, a personal sense of "at oneness" with a transcendent force?

From the perspective of a theology of sexuality, we wonder what contribution the experience of the traditional housewife/priestess makes to a woman's ability to form the bond of "two in one flesh." What hints about the steps necessary for any type of human relationship can be found in her experience?

Reflecting on our analysis of the traditional housewife/priestess we are reminded of the various interpretations the story of Martha and Mary has received over the centuries. This multi-leveled story reveals new challenges and understandings of human relationships and behavior when interpreted from the perspective of a theology of sexuality and from our analysis of the housewife/priestess.

Certainly Mary, as did all women of her time, engaged in the traditional role of the housewife/priestess and undoubtedly helped create an environment in which the guest, Jesus, was made to feel at home. But, for her, part of this being "at home" included her physical presence and attention to the guest, showing an awareness of the personhood of the guest over and above his need for physical sustenance.

Martha was chided not because, as many interpretations have implied, housework is an inferior activity, but because her compulsion with housework led her to succumb to its demonic potential and to ignore her guest. Martha, like the disciples, failed to recognize the transcendent possibilities of her ordinary environment. Despite her attention to the details of housework, those who entered her home did not experience it as sacred space because her attention to the details of housework did not allow her to be open to them and their personal needs. And her complaints about Mary's inactivity show that she derived little satisfaction from her role.

This interpretation views both Martha and Mary as traditional housewives/priestesses but sees the creation of an environment where people will feel "at home" as possible only when the housewife is open to others. This is the transcendent possibility of the house-wife's worth.

Thus, this experience of openness to others which is part and parcel of the positive dimensions of the experience of the tradition-al housewife/priestess may be the missing ingredient in the experi-ences of many women who enter the work force at every level not just in the board room. There is excitement and challenge in the competi-tion of the work world of our marketing manager, and there is the per-sonal satisfaction of an income, but there is little of the personal response to her particular skill or talent in her experience as an en-tertainer and a gourmet cook. Her role in the questing world beyond the home, while monetarily and even personally satisfying in many ways, does not seem to offer the same mystical possibilities -- openness to others -- that she felt in her role as traditional housewife/priestess.

The experiences of the traditional housewife/priestess suggest that, if our activity is linked with a concern for persons, then the world in which we perform our daily ritual can be transformed into a a sacred space where we face ultimate questions. The ritualistic housework of the housewife/priestess in her mode of waiting offered this possibility to many women. This feminine characteristic of caring and concern for others, nurtured in the experience of the traditional housewife/priestess, needs to be considered more fully by women as a positive contribution they can make as they move into roles other than that of the traditional housewife/priestess.

This dimension of human experience which has for the most part been practiced by women must be appreciated and celebrated by women so that it may be shared with men and contribute to opportunities for bonding between men and women. When both a man and a woman respond to the bonding challenge rooted in the sexual attraction of the body, they will be more successful in this unity if they both appreciate the need for care and concern for the other which is at the root of the mystical possibility of the experience of the traditional housewife/priestess. The bond a man and a woman form, based on this mutual concern and care, will then serve as a model for other human relationships. Individuals in such unions will carry this experience into other relationships; couples will model the benefits of such a relationship for their children and for others they encounter.

As our analysis of the traditional housewife/priestess indicates, a pastoral theology of femininity must be rooted in a careful examination of the various activities of women, both past and present, as a way of appreciating the positive contribution their experiences, which have often been considered inferior, make to an understanding of human nature. Today's woman is confronted with a situation in which the role of traditional housewife/priestess, with its task of creating an environment in which others may feel "at home," is being called into question. Women who have lived a mode of waiting are moving into a mode of questing, leaving a void as the sacred space of the home loses its priestess who kept the home fires burning. Humans need a place "to come home to," a place where they can develop their self-awareness, where they can feel "at home." The task of the traditional housewife/priestess who created such an environment perhaps no longer needs to be performed only by women, but the experience of giving and receiving care and concern is still necessary for the development of self-awareness. The task of caring and showing concern for others must continue to be performed.

The challenge for modern women becomes how to share this task with others and also how to bring this sense of care and concern into the world of questing. If women who move into the work force can bring the skills of a Mary who measures her "success" by her ability to be a gift to another person, rather than the attitudes of a Martha there is a possibility they can challenge the world of questing to be more human. The role of the traditional housewife/priestess evolved because a woman's body with its reproductive possibilities kept her attached to the home. The challenge for today's woman is to uncover all the positive aspects of humanness nurtured during a period of overemphasis on the reproductive possibilities of sexuality. Many of these aspects might be of assistance in a time when we have rediscovered the revelatory possibilities of the bonding aspects of human sexuality. According to the Divine Plan, the unity of a man and a woman is to be a revelation of Divine Love. Women have been caretakers of many aspects of this Divine Love in their role as housewives. These aspects must not be lost in their transition to a new role.

Sharing the task of creating the home as sacred space could lead to the creation of a group of househusbands/priests. This would offer men the opportunity to uncover new insights into human nature not acquired in their questing endeavors or in women's waiting. This sharing would have to go beyond the mere dividing up of household tasks; it would have to encourage men to take responsibility for the creation of a "place to come home to," allowing them to contribute to an appreciation of what that means.

Just as women have learned to develop many talents and abilities they never knew they had until they entered the world of questing, allowing them to bring feminine insights into that world, men need to consider what masculine insights they can bring to the world of waiting. We hope that the feminine influence will help "humanize" the world of questing. Certainly men in their world of questing have nurtured aspects of humanness that could contribute, in turn, to a more "humanized" home as sacred space.

Presently both the angry Catholic woman and those "feminists" who are not angry at the Church are forced to work out their response to the situation of women with little support from their Church. Without a vision of the personhood of woman, rooted in a Christian understanding of sexuality, all Catholic women will miss the support their religion offers for their search for a deeper understanding and appreciation of femininity.

Pastoral theologians and church leaders who support the need for celebrating the revelatory potential of femininity might not affect the imagination of alienated "feminists" with their abstract statements. Still, if a Church is committed to helping women clarify the ambiguity they experience when they sense a "loss" of the mystical potential of the housewife/priestess, then that Church will help create an environment where women are able to appreciate how deeply their

femininity has contributed to an understanding of humanness. Once women no longer feel that femininity equals inferiority, they will be
more included to live out the positive aspects of that femininity in
whatever work they perform. Then their "anger" might diminish.

Given the complexity of the religious imagination, even those
church leaders who accept the premise of this chapter might wonder
how to break the often unconscious cycle of image generation. Before
examining how local church, with good pastoral leadership and lay responsibility, might contribute to the task of image formation, we
will examine the importance of a theology of marriage for our
concerns.

CHAPTER XIII: THEOLOGY OF MARRIAGE

If the Church is to overcome the negative image of its support for stereotypic roles for women, another area of theological reflection which it must revise is that of marriage. For the most part, a "theology of marriage" has been captive of the reproductive needs of previous human cultures. Much of what passed for a theology of marriage in the past was in reality an attempt to interpret rules concerning valid marriages. Eventually, that which made a marriage sacramental and incapable of being put asunder was a union of two baptized persons in the presence of the church's minister which was then lawfully consummated in the first act of marital intercourse. Such a union was until "death do us part."

Eileen Zieget Silbermann in her book, The Savage Sacrament[1], calls for a dialogue between Christian feminists and post-Vatican II theologians (most probably an impossible task given the tendency of the former to ideology and of the latter to abstraction). She maintains that a viable theology of marriage will be forthcoming only when theologians, who in the past have not listened to woman's experience, take it into consideration in developing a perspective on marriage. While I do not disagree with the necessity to include woman's experience in theological reflection, it is perhaps more valid to say that most theological discussion of marriage has been limited by its lack of consideration of the experience of marriage in the lives of both the men and the women who are married.

Certainly until the most recent past, at least within the Catholic tradition, all discussions of the theology of marriage were the work of celibate men, many of whom had little contact with married people. For these theologians the legalistic approach, based on a consideration of marriage as a contract, seemed to offer ample support for lifelong fidelity. When the couple was physically faithful, the marriage was a faithful sign of the relationship between God and the church. Adultery was a sin against the marriage contract because it was a sharing of one's body with a person other than the marital spouse (see A Feast of Love for a detailed analysis of Pope John Paul II's distinction between adultery in the body and adultery in the heart). Love as an intimacy relationship between two persons, each unique and unrepeatable in the sight of God, never entered into these discussions. A man who did not commit adultery was considered a faithful spouse even if he related to his wife only as a sex object. Women were led to believe that they were faithful as long as they remained with their spouse even if they avoided any emotional involvement with their husbands.

The chief reason for this narrow approach to a theology of marriage can be found in a lack of understanding of the mystery of human sexuality and of its pervasiveness in all aspects of our lives, not merely the physical. A theology of sexuality calls for a bonding of two in one flesh as gift and source of revelation of God to each other. Such a theology would encourage the development of intimacy—that is the sharing of identities—between a husband and a wife, a sharing that takes place only when the husband and wife relate to each other as individual persons, not as stereotypes.

Investigating the situation of angry Catholic women led to a discovery of a greater alienation from the Church among some housewives than among some non-housewives. This calls us to examine the contribution a Church, be it the universal church or the local parish, can make to the image of man in the workplace and woman in the home. Certainly in the 1950's the message brides-to-be received in marriage preparation courses and pre-Cana was that a working wife was a detriment to marital satisfaction. The ideal was the wife who ceased working at the time of her marriage; an exception was made if her working did not interfere with plans for a family and if the mother did not return to work after the birth of her child. Couples were advised to save the wife's income so as to avoid reliance on two incomes. Women were encouraged to pursue an education that would make them good wives and mothers -- possibly with skills that could be exercised in the event of a husband's illness or death but that would allow them to continue their role as homemaker (teaching, nursing, freelance writing, for example).

The Catholic system of marriage preparation and educational programs emphasized that it was a man's world and woman's place was in the home. Good Catholic women did not postpone the birth of their first child in order to pursue a career or secure financial gain. It is little wonder that some of these women experience conflict as they face the opportunity to assume additional roles but lack the skills and the encouragement from their husbands who still cite a religious support for the conviction that women should not be free to exercise talents and abilities in the work world.

Often a husband's support is crucial for a woman's search for an identity as a person in the 1980's, whether she chooses to combine family and career or to dedicate herself to the art of homemaking, possibly engaging in volunteer activities when homemaking demands less of her time. There is a tremendous amount of guilt among women during this period of transition; guilt because they are not working and don't seem to their friends to be using their talents, or guilt because they are working and are caught between commitment to family and commitment to work. A husband plays a supportive role in helping a woman overcome these guilt feelings though this is not always easy for a man, especially when he, too, experiences confusion over changing sex roles and expectations for husband/wife relationships. Many marital relationships suffer from the inability of a husband and wife to address the inevitable conflicts caused by changing roles.

Unfortunately, the theology of marriage based on the canon law view of marriage as a contract does not offer a religious challenge to a couple facing these problems. Silbermann entitles her book on a theology of marriage The Savage Sacrament because "for many women marriage is a savage sacrament," meaning that it is "fierce, ferocious, cruel." Many women, in her view, experience marriage as "pernicious and destructive," and, undoubtedly, although Silbermann does not discuss this, many men also find marriage pernicious and destructive. Neither Catholic women nor Catholic men have heard the challenge of marriage as an intimacy relationship in which two people strive to share their identities as they journey through marriage to a deeper appreciation of God. They do not hear the call to overcome the destructiveness possible in a marriage.

A theology of marriage rooted in a theology of sexuality in which the bonding of "two in one flesh"--is a revelation of God, should be at the basis of church teaching on marriage, and its instruction for pre-marriage and ongoing marriage education. This theology of marriage is also rooted in the experience of marriage in a societal situation where there is an increased awareness of the possibility of intimacy between a husband and wife.

Once a culture gives up its excessive concern with reproductive survival, the desire for intimacy in a marital relationship becomes an important goal. Indeed, generative reproduction where parents are able to care for the personhood of their offspring demands that the parents have a relationship which respects each other's personhood and is a genuine attempt to share their identities (personhoods) in a relationship of intimacy. Thus, a pastoral theology of marriage rooted in the experience of marriage and in a theology of sexuality is responsive to both these roots when it is a theology of marital intimacy.

The process of correlating the experience of marital intimacy and the theology of sexuality so as to develop a theology of marital intimacy requires an analysis of the struggle for marital intimacy. A correlation of that analysis with the images and stories of our faith clarifies some of the ambiguities of the experience.

A group of social scientists and theologians, including the authors of this book, used this process in a colloquium on human intimacy which emphasized the importance of developing a vision which would speak to the religious imagination of married people.[2] The ability to imagine the possibility of intimacy in marriage is a prerequisite for overcoming the inevitable obstacles that will occur over the lifetime of a marriage in the modern world. If our faith tradition, through its symbols and stories, can challenge and support marital partners in the cultivation of the image of a good marriage, then a couple will be more inclined to appreciate both the gift and the virtue of "purity of heart." They will experience the grace (gift) of the Spirit as an assistance in their search for marital intimacy (virtue).

The experience of marital intimacy can be described as a journey of a man and a woman, a journey which has sexual, psychological and religious dimensions. As a man and woman strive for physical and psychological intimacy -- a sharing of mind and bodies -- they inevitably encounter Mystery which requires a religious clarification. From a religious perspective, this journey of marital intimacy can be viewed as a major dimension of the partners' search for the ultimate meaning of life. The journey of marital intimacy is also a journey toward a deeper and richer appreciation of the Divine Being who "created us male and female in the image of God."

In the colloquium, we reflected on this journey of marital intimacy in a modern technological society where marriages of fifty years and more are becoming more common. We grappled with the inevitable obstacles a couple will encounter over this fifty year period, obstacles which seriously challenge the partners' ability to live out a commitment of intimacy, a commitment the psychologists tell us is part-and-parcel of the healthy growth and development of a mature individual. And we considered how the stories of our faith challenge us to "imagine" growth in marital intimacy.

Our analysis of marital intimacy noted its cyclical nature. Most couples go through numerous cycles during the lifetime of their marriage, repeating over and over again the stages of falling in love, settling down, bottoming out and beginning again. Growth and development within a marital relationship, occurs when the cycles of marital intimacy form a spiral rather than a continual circle. Each time marital partners begin again, they achieve more depth in their sexual, psychological and religious intimacy. They experience the gift of the Spirit, the "purity of heart" which comes to those who participate in the continuing redemption offered by Jesus. Each individual experience of growth in marital intimacy offers those who wish to examine it an opportunity to discover God's presence in the experience and, at the same time, to reveal the God found in that experience.

Our religious tradition calls upon us to embrace the possibility that a marital relationship is a reflection of God. In addition to the Genesis revelation of the "two in one flesh" being "in the image of God," we find numerous Old Testament references to Yahweh's longing for a relationship with Israel that would be a model of marital intimacy. Israel is repeatedly chided for her failure as a spouse (Hosea). St. Paul reminds the Ephesians that marriage is somehow a sign of the union between Christ and the Church (Ephesians 5:32) and, although the Church did not officially proclaim marriage as one of the seven sacraments until the Council of Trent, from its earliest beginning there was an acknowledgement that marriage has a sacramental character -- that is, marriage continues to reveal God in every time and every place.

We look to the images and stories of our faith tradition for an inspiration that will spark the imagination of marital partners as they move through the highs and lows of their journey to marital intimacy. In so doing, we are struck by how the continuing theme of death and resurrection speaks to the process necessary for beginning again in a marital relation-ship. As anyone who has been married, or who has observed the experience of marriage, knows, the excitement of the initial experience of falling in love soon gives way to the necessary accommodations of daily living. In time the "romance" of falling in love seems lost, and one or both partners yearns for "something more" in the relationship. Misunderstandings which often accompany an unevenness of interest in this search for "something more" leads to the conflicts of the bottoming out of a relationship, a bot-toming out which can trigger an end to the relationship, or a static no-growth situation or a decision to give up (die to) the habits of the settling down stage which have stifled the passion of romantic love. This latter decision paves the way for the grace of beginning again. When we examine each stage of a cycle of marital intimacy, we discover the inter-connectedness of the psychological, physical and religious dimensions of the experience.

Falling in love is the tremendously exciting response to the powerful physical attraction of man for woman and woman for man which was put there by God so we humans might be "in the image of God." This attraction is meant to encourage humans to form bonding relationships that assured the survival of the species. During a period of falling in love we are like Adam and Eve discovering each other in the Garden, and like the Israelites in Egypt at Mount Sinai who discover a lover who will treat them royally and never stop pursuing them. Like the lovers in the "Song of Songs," we yearn for our lover during an absence, finding that a romantic fantasy sen-sitizes us to the salvitic power of the other. We tend to ignore our lov-er's shortcomings because like Yahweh, in Paddy Chayefsky's play Gideon, for us "passion has no reason." The gift of love bestowed upon us by our lover draws us out of ourselves and offers us a wonderful experience of the grace of a God who created both of us so we could be gift to each other.

Though, undoubtedly, there is some sharing of ideas during the period of falling in love on topics such as woman's role, the power of our passionate love generally blinds us to any inconsistencies between our two experiences of male and female lifestyles.

With the settling down in the early stages of marriage we begin to get to know each other more intimately both psychologically and physically and, during this stage, have the opportunity to develop habits that will help us grow in both sexual and psychological intimacy. Here we are like Adam and Eve becoming familiar with the Garden, the Israelites turning the promised land into a powerful nation and the disciples of Jesus tending to the nitty-gritty of everyday life with their wandering rabbi.

The inevitability of settling down in any relationship has both positive and negative aspects. It is difficult to share identity when the other is part of our romantic fantasies and doesn't have a "real" identity, just as it is difficult to develop an ease at sexual intimacy without the freedom to relate to the other as "another self" in a relationship of commitment. Though settling down is an important ingredient in any relationship, it inevitably leads to the condition of "taking for granted," in which the marital partners, consciously or unconsciously, build walls which stop the journey of growth in marital intimacy. At this point stereotypic expectations for male/female behavior begin to substitute for regard for person.

Bottoming out occurs for a variety of reasons, some of which are primarily psychological and others which are primarily physical, but all of which are most often related to an inability to realize that the grace of our masculinity and femininity holds us to an intertwining of our physical and psychological identities so that "two in one flesh" will be "in the image of God." Our journey of marital intimacy requires a commitment to simultaneous growth in both areas.

The quest for psychological intimacy should encourage us to be more skilled as physical lovers just as increased skill in sexual intimacy challenges us to a similar sharing of minds and hearts. When either or both are lacking, the marital partners become like Adam and Eve hiding from God, like Israel in Babylon or like the disciples feeling shame over their denial of Jesus. We have lost the grace of falling in love, and generally, both physical and psychological intimacy are unsatisfying and filled with hostility. The spouse who was trusted has let us down and we begin to wonder about our own failure. The mourning we experience at the death of our romantic fantasies, if we allow it to remind us of the wonderful grace of romantic love, can be a call to rediscover that love.

If a marital relationship is to be a journey in intimacy, the mourning of the bottoming out stage is a necessary prelude to beginning again, to a renewed commitment to the original promises of falling in love, though now newly enriched by the awareness of ourself and the other that has developed during the stages of settling down and bottoming out. Each of the marital partners must abandon those barriers set up to avoid true openness in the relationship. The "naked and not afraid" of Genesis II requires a continual willingness to die to those things which separate us.

110

Happily, for most people, the lure of our bodies, the attraction of man for woman and woman for man which led us to fall in love, continues to exert some power during the bottoming out stage, and the loss of sexual intimacy often triggers the initiative to begin again, to honestly face what it is that led to the horror of bottoming out. We emerge from bottoming out changed by the experience and called to a growth that will once again give us the rapture of falling in love. The grace of our sexuality, the call to bonding, is a grace of Creation recaptured in Redemption and continued in the gift of the Holy Spirit. We develop "purity of heart" when in our relationship of marital intimacy we respond to this grace and begin again by addressing the issues which separate us. One of the issues which causes conflict in many marriages today and which must be faced over and over again as partners move through cycles of marital intimacy, is the issue of male/female roles and husband/wife roles. By emphasizing the sacramental sign of intimacy, a theology of marital intimacy is closely related to a theology of sexuality which views male and female relationships based on stereotypes as adultery; it challenges partners who are beginning again to be open to the bonding grace of their sexuality. When stereotypes contribute to an image of husband and wife, they are as adulterous as an act of physical unfaithfulness. The challenge to grow in intimacy is a challenge to relate to the particular person of our spouse. In the case of a woman who is searching for a positive image in this time of changing roles, a spouse who refuses to join with her in that search sets up obstacles which must be removed if the marriage is to begin again.

We have seen that a search for marital intimacy entails a continual death and resurrection. We must die to the all too easy tendency to neglect the personhood of our spouse; we must rise to a joy we discover as each of us unearths new facets of our personality, facets which might never have come to light without the grace-filled presence of our spouse urging us to overcome the inevitable obstacles and difficulties to personal and marital growth.

A theology which emphasizes the importance of intimacy would be of assistance to pastoral workers who are aware of the conflict in many marriages stemming from confusion over changing sex roles. A husband who does not support his wife in a search for a valid identity in these changing times is unable to reveal God as a Lover. A wife who, in her search for a valid identity, refuses to consider her relationship to her spouse as part of this search, is also failing to be a sign of Divine Love to her spouse, rendering the marriage incapable of becoming a relationship of intimacy.

The importance of intimacy for religious experience is evident when we consider the situation of angry Catholic women. The positive impact of "feminism" on sexual fulfillment, especially among younger marrieds where both the "feminism" of the husband and the "feminism" of the wife are effective, plus the husband's ability to suppress negative attitudes towards Church, give some indication that for a segment of American Catholic women marital intimacy allows a spouse to reveal the love of God.

The alienation of certain Catholic "feminists" demands an understanding of marriage that will encourage both men and women to give up false images of their roles in life. The "two in one flesh" of unique and unrepeatable persons sharing their identities in a relationship of intimacy does not preclude the possibility of individuals developing their own talents and abilities. But the sharing of a marital relationship, a physical and psychological nakedness, requires a willingness to be gift to each other. As Pope John Paul II points out, this giftedness of the relationship of intimacy is the direct opposite of a relationship of appropriation where one or the other spouse "lords it over" a mate, forcing the other to act out of preconceived stereotypic notions of husband or wife.

A theology of marital intimacy which recognizes that for the majority of humankind, the search for intimacy is integral to the search for God should lead to the creation of new images of marriage. These new images might help eradicate the negative images of the Church held by angry Catholic women. In a relationship of intimacy, the spouse who wishes to grow in intimacy helps reveal God as Lover when he helps his wife choose wisely among the many opportunities available to her in today's world.

Church leaders and pastoral workers hoping to alleviate the anger of alienated Catholic "feminists" can ill afford to ignore the religious dimension of the search for intimacy. They must learn to challenge husbands and wives to see that stereotypic role expectations are obstacles to intimacy. They must remind marital partners of their ability to reveal God for each other, establishing a model for other relationships.

For some Catholic "feminists" the experience of marriage contributes to a positive experience of Church. To better understand how this occurs we now must turn to a consideration of the relationship between the experience of God in marriage and family life and the experience of God found in the institutional church.

CHAPTER XIV: THE DOMESTIC CHURCH

The basic argument underlying this book is that the imagination level of religion, rather than the theological level, is the definitive influence on religious behavior. Thus, theological arguments are insufficient for the "conversion" of a woman whose religious imagination has been deeply influenced by negative experiences of Church as the supporter of traditional woman's roles to the detriment of modern woman's search for identity. Although we have explored how a positive theology of sexuality in its view of the personhood of women, along with a theology of marriage based on this interpretation of sexuality, should lead to the Church being a strong supporter of woman's quest for identity, we know that theological argumentation does not affect the religious imagination. The salesman in the coffee shop, the 1950's college graduate and women who fit our category of "feminist" will not be swayed until they have an experience of church which counteracts their present negative image.

If we hope to have the theological ideas discussed in the previous three chapters influence the religious imagination of alienated women, we need, first of all, to consider the image of "Church" as it is perceived by many people. In analyzing why this image is often different than the theological image of "the people of God" invoked by Vatican II, we become aware of the gap between that theological image and the reality of the church experience of many Catholics, most particularly women. We will then consider another image developed briefly at Vatican II and elaborated somewhat in the apostolic exhortation on the family, <u>Familiaris</u> <u>Consortio</u>-- the "domestic church." The evidence of the sociological investigation of angry Catholic women suggests that a deeper appreciation of the concept of "domestic church" might supply an avenue for religious leaders and pastoral workers who would hope to translate a theology of sexuality into a positive support for women's quest for identity.

First of all, let us consider the term "Church." Despite initial eloquent support for the conciliar concept of the Church as the "people of God," the majority of people I encounter from a wide range of backgrounds -- academic theologians, bishops, parish priests, pastoral workers, lay Catholics, Protestant observers of the Church, and the media -- still mean the hierarchical institutional church when they speak of <u>the Church</u>. Even Catholics who, because of disagreement with the institutional Church, no longer participate in religious practices on a regular basis, do not see that the image "people of God" could also include them in the Church. Even for those who might still consider themselves Catholic, anger at the Church is aimed at the institution.

Much of the conflict in the Church today between the Pope and bishops, between bishops and priests, between pastors and lay people, is the result of this incompatibility between an image of the Church as a "people of God," (which in an American context suggests something bordering on democracy), and the reality of the continuation of the clerical, hierarchical model of church, in some instances and in some places with all the negative connotations applicable to that model. We might say to the angry Catholic woman, "But you are the Church; you as part of the 'people of God' have an important contribution to make to the continuation of Christ's presence in the modern world which is, after all, the real reason for the existence of the Church." And the angry Catholic woman would most likely laugh in our face because the reality of the situation is that she feels little, if any, ability to influence the institutional structure of the Church.

There undoubtedly have been attempts to institute a conciliar model of Church in relationships between pastors and lay people, between bishops and priests, between the Pope and bishops. Still, there are a sufficient number of instances of hierarchical clericalism (in all the perjorative sense of that word), even at times among those who profess to practice a conciliar "people of God" model. It is no wonder that the alienated Catholic of whatever sex holds on to images which, at least in theory, are not part of the post-Vatican II Church.

And women who have been strongly influenced by the hierarchical, clerical image of Church find it even more difficult to imagine themselves as the Church, as the "people of God," as co-sharers with all the other members of the Church, including priests, bishops and Pope, in spreading the Good News in the modern world. The structures of the institutional church do not easily lend themselves to creating an image of equality among its membership. The traditional barring of women from key leadership roles open only to ordained ministers—thus barring women from these roles—does little to convey the impression that the personhood of women is on a level equal to the personhood of men.

Certainly since the Second Vatican Council, many new roles have opened for women in the Church; indeed, at least in the United States, it is difficult to imagine how many active parishes would survive without the professional assistance of women in education and other non-ordained forms of ministry as well as in volunteer activities. Still, the denial of ordination to women creates a problem for a Church which still operates out of a clerical, hierarchical model even though it is an updated, post Vatican II form of the model.

The fact of the matter is that women are denied access to what one priest I know calls "the Priest's Club." A new bishop comes to a diocese and inevitably his principal advisors are drawn from the ranks of the priests in the diocese, perhaps a few influential laymen, and nowadays a token woman or two, but the crucial first task of the bishop seems to be directly related to communication with the priests, a group to which women do not belong. And in his day-to-day functioning in a diocese, a bishop generally surrounds himself with clerical assistants who interpret for him the needs of the diocese. Priorities for the diocese are filtered through priests' senates and clerical advisors much more forcefully than through special interest lay groups or through women's groups.

So, too, a new pastor comes to a parish and his principal advisors are the rectory staff, perhaps with some consultation with parish council and school staff. But the nitty gritty of getting to know the new parish goes on in rectory conversations from which women are omitted.

Women wanting to be a significant voice in Church discussions are somewhat similar to the lay dean of a college run by a religious order: "If I could only get into their refectory at dinner each evening, I'd be in a better position to influence things around here. All these consultations, trustee meetings and the like, are just window dressing. I'm convinced that the real decisions about this university are made over cocktails and dinner each evening." All but the most naive women recognize they are excluded from most of the important decision-making situations in the parish, diocesan and universal Church. At the same time, when the Church fails to include women in its deliberations at every level, it suffers from a lack of appreciation of the feminine dimension of human experience.

In addition, the denial of ordination to women, along with the refusal to allow women to perform acolyte functions during liturgies, reinforces the image that women are somehow second class citizens. When our youngest daughter was in sixth grade, she told me that she replied to the parish priest's question of why did she think he wanted to bring all of the boys of that grade together with the answer, "to talk about altar girls." She then proceeded to ask me, in a truly remarkable display of angry Irish womanhood, "Where in the Bible does it say that little girls can't be altar boys?" (I might add that none of her four older sisters or her mother had ever discussed this topic with her.) Her altar girl campaign gained a slight momentum among her female classmates when the girls learned that there would be a monetary reward for every funeral or wedding served. But their enthusiasm was quickly squelched, not only by church authorities, but also by little boys who did not want little girls interfering on their turf. Sixth grade girls could handle the ire of the boys, but by the time they reached seventh and eighth grade -- and the parish staff made half-hearted attempts to include them in some fashion as altar servers--the beginnings of boy-girl relationships and the possibility of being ostracized for "feminist" behavior killed much of the girls' enthusiasm. I don't know what image these young women now have of

Church, but I suspect that they realize that there are some areas of Church where they might fear to tread lest they be put in their proper place.

Why is it that some women experience this incongruity between the image of the Church as the "people of God" and the reality of woman's place in the Church and still continue active involvement in the Church, while others see this incongruity as a reason to divorce themselves from the institutional church and, in some instances, even to go so far as to sever all relationships with patriarchal religions? We could say that many women do not seek a different role in the Church. They would categorize themselves as "non-feminists" and see no reason for the Church to change its stance regarding women.

However, many "feminists," and even some Feminists who continue to work within the structures of the institutional church hoping, oftentimes it seems to them hoping against hope, to bring about changes in the church structure. They recognize that the present situation of the Church is closely linked to a cultural situation in which both Church and culture supported traditional roles for the sake of survival of the society. They realize that the Church is still caught in a traditional mode and they hope to bring about a change in the institutional Church. While they do not reject the idea of the Church as the "people of God"--indeed their aim is to make the reality of church life more in tune with that image--they admit that the image does not fit their experience of the Church. They feel that if the image were explored more fully, it would be a forceful supporter of the recognition of the personhood of women. From the evidence of our sociological investigation, it would seem that some influence outside the hierarchical clerical structure of the Church has suppressed the negative effects this structure could have on these women's image of themselves.

If we move from the theological level to the religious imagination level in our consideration of the idea of Church, we discover another level of Church in our experience, a level which is often only indirectly influenced by theological discussions and institutional policies. As our analysis of the experience of the angry Catholic woman indicates, our respondents initially perceived the institutional Church's attitudes on women's role through their mothers' degree of adherence to the model supported by the Church. Additionally, it appears that even when that initial perception might be expected to cause negative feelings for a "feminist" woman, her spouse can be a suppressor of this negative response. These findings reinforce those of Professor McCready which indicate that our families—those of birth and those of later years—are a powerful influence on our values and on our religious behavior.

The family—be it only a husband and wife discovering and revealing God in their journey of marital intimacy or the larger unit where "with the help of the Lord" (Genesis 4) spouses interact with each other and with children—is the primary level of influence on the religious imagination. The influence of family on religious practices and values was highlighted many years ago in the original National Opinion Research Center study on the effects of Catholic education, which found that education in the schools reinforced the values acquired in the home, and in Professor McCready's findings on the influence of a marital partner on one's religious practices.

Though the family has undoubtedly always played a role as a religious influence, its influence is perhaps more apparent, and possibly even stronger, in this period of upheaval following the Second Vatican Council when many Catholics no longer felt the need to follow strict proscriptions of church laws in order to avoid eternal damnation. Our salesman felt that all church rules were of equal insignificance in nurturing religious growth. Since it was no longer necessary for his eternal salvation that he abstain from meat on Friday, it also seemed unnecessary to attend church on Sunday. Unfortunately, in the transition from a Church of rules to a Church of the "people of God," he never heard of the value of community worship or else never had the opportunity to experience this value for himself. No one has touched his religious imagination.

Church leaders wishing to speak to the anger of alienated Catholic women and hoping to avoid this anger in future generations of women would be well advised to address their attention to the reality of the family influence on the religious imagination. Only then will they be able to overcome the problems of a clerical, hierarchical model of Church even as the Church moves to a more collegial model of operation. Pastoral theologians who seek to correlate the experience of women with the richness of the Catholic Christian tradition must find a way to increase our appreciation of the important influence of family on religious imagination and religious practices.

There is another theological understanding of Church, briefly alluded to at the Second Vatican Council but barely discussed after that until it was referred to again in the apostolic exhortation on the family following the Synod on the Family. Our investigation of the religious imagination would indicate that this understanding of "domestic church" is quite appropriate for the reality of religion in our lives. The concept of the "domestic church" (<u>Lumen Gentium</u>, 10; <u>Apostolicam Acuositatem</u>, 10: <u>Familiaris Consortio</u>, 4) recognizes that there is a level of church other than that of the hierarchical institutional church.

Unfortunately, due to negative publicity regarding some sections of the apostolic exhortation, the report of the Synod on the Family has not been widely discussed at the level of the local church. Although pastoral ministers will acknowledge the importance of the family and family life ministers speak of the important task of returning religious education to the family, the current discussion of the family in the Church is rooted neither in an understanding of the influence of the family on the religious imagination nor in an appreciation of the revelatory possibilities of family experience. Pope John Paul II touches on these possibilities when he refers to the individual family as a "church in miniature," a "living image, an historical representation of the mystery of Church" (FC. 49).

When correlated with an appreciation of the family as the basic former of the religious imagination, the theology of the "domestic church," spelled out in <u>Familiaris Consortio</u>, helps to clarify some of the confusion we encounter when we try to understand the anger of the alienated Catholic. At the same time, the pastoral theology developed in response to this process of correlation challenges church leaders and pastoral ministers to recognize that the religious level of Church has more influence on a person's ability to experience God and salvation than the theological level and institutional level.

122

For the purposes of our study of angry Catholic women, we will correlate the theology of the "domestic church" outlined in Familiaris
Consortio with the experience of family in our modern technological culture, with particular emphasis on how family socializes its members to attitudes, values and behaviors regarding the role of women. This process
of pastoral theology touches on a limited area of family experience, but
specific application of abstract theological reflection is necessary if we
are to uncover ways in which there can be interaction between the religious imagination level and the theological level of an experience of
faith. Abstract theological statements on the family as "domestic church"
are only valid if, in fact, the family is able to influence the religious
imagination of its members. At the same time, the possibility
of experiencing the family as "domestic church" calls for a vision of
family life which clarifies the ambiguity of the various facets of family
through references to our faith tradition.

In Familiaris Consortio Pope John Paul II examines the bonds between the Church and the Christian family. As the family fulfills its
ecclesial task, it serves the building up of the Kingdom of God in history. Through the sacrament of marriage the Christian family receives the
love of Christ, becoming a saved community, at the same time that it is
called to communicate Christ's love to others, thus becoming a saving
community (FC. 49). The family has a specific and original ecclesial role
when, as an intimate community of life and love, it places itself at the
service of the Church and of society. The family participates in the prophetic, priestly and kingly mission of Christ and of his church when, as a
community of love, it goes about its everyday task (FC. 50).

123

The Christian family builds up the Kingdom of God when it is 1) a believing and evangelizing community, 2) a community in dialogue with God
and 3) a community at the service of humankind (FC 51-64). This vision of
the Christian family correlates with the sociological understanding of the
family as the place where individuals are socialized into values, attitudes and behaviors; it acknowledges the role of the family as the most important influence for the formation of religious imagination and for
religious behavior and calls upon family to recognize this role as a way
to continue the work of Christ in this time and in this place.

When we apply the challenge of this vision of the "domestic church"
to a consideration of the ways in which a family consciously or unconsciously influences values, attitudes and behaviors regarding sexuality,
marriage and women's role, we see how important it is that this first line
of influence on the religious imagination be conscious of its fundamental
ecclesial task.

As the "domestic church," the Christian family has the prophetic role
of welcoming and announcing the word of God which it does when it functions as a believing and evangelizing community (FC 51-54). As the family, consciously or unconsciously, influences the formation of the
religious imagination, it reveals (announces) the basic beliefs about the
meaning of life discovered in the interactions of the family members and
contributes to the formation of attitudes and behaviors related to these
beliefs. Beliefs about the body, sexuality, stereotypic roles and marital
intimacy are acquired, often unconsciously, through the example of our parents and reinforced, or sometimes changed, by the example and expectation
of our spouse. When a man and a woman see their marital relationship as a

124

journey into a deeper appreciation of God, they are challenged to a conscious awareness of how they influence each other and their children. If they appreciate their bodies and their sexual attraction as a lure to a bonding whereby they come to a better appreciation of Divine Love, they will "evangelize" their children to a Christian attitude regarding sexuality, "the basic fact of human existence."

The research on angry Catholic women underscores the influence a mother's lifestyle has on her daughter's ability to develop an identity and continue religious practices, an indication that the "evangelization" that takes place in a family can be either positive or negative. Regarding appropriate behavior on sexuality-related issues, the Christian family is similar to the crowd gathered around Jesus hearing the Pharisees being directed to turn to the "beginning" and uncover the Divine Plan for human sexuality (Matthew 14). When parents and spouses take seriously a theology of bonding and a theology of marital intimacy and learn to celebrate the personhood of each family member by recognizing the valuable contribution each makes, they also set the stage for "evangelizing" others beyond the family.

In addition to its prophetic role, the Christian family has a priestly role whereby, as a community in dialogue with God, it is called to be sanctified and to sanctify the ecclesial community in the world (FC. 55-62). The sacraments of Marriage, the Eucharist and Reconciliation are constant reminders of this priestly task. The grace of the sacrament of Marriage accompanies the couple throughout their life. The Eucharist reminds them again of Christ's covenant with the Church, the source of their own marital covenant. Reconciliation assists them with the repentance and mutual pardon which are a part of daily family life. In addition, family prayer, which has for its object family life itself, enhances the "dignity and responsibility of the Christian family as the "domestic church" which can be achieved only with God's unceasing aid."

The way in which the family dialogues with God certainly plays a crucial role in the formation of the religious imagination. The occasions in which the family gathers for liturgical celebration and prayer certainly reflect the image of God that is developed within the family. Indeed, oftentimes, a non-liturgical celebration of joy or gathering of the family in time of sadness leads to a recognition of God's presence in our midst and turns the experience into a prayer. Research evidence indicates a strong link between a family celebration of Christmas and Easter, with its stories of the cave of Bethlehem and the cave on Easter morn, and a person's ability to perceive God as a "Lover." The celebration of important liturgical events, as well as important family experiences, reminds the family members of God's presence in their midst; it also encourages in them the development of an image of God which reflects the beliefs enshrined in the family.

If deeply rooted negative attitudes on sexuality and the personhood of woman have contributed to the disposition toward Church of the angry Catholic woman, then it seems imperative that one task of a family's dialogue with God be its consideration (or re-consideration) of its attitudes, values and behaviors regarding the body and sexuality. If the God who is dialogued with, celebrated and prayed to in the family is the loving, passionate Creator God of Genesis, of the redemption of the Body and of the Holy Spirit, not only women but all family members will experience the liberation of the body. If repentance and forgiveness are experienced in the family, then we come to know something of a God who might say "passion has no reason." When a family remembers the various liturgical celebrations which honor Mary, it emphasizes the revelation of God in the various facets of the experience of a particular woman. Through these activities, the family can help apply the virtues of Mary's life to the experiences both women and men encounter as they go about the task of sanctifying the ecclesial community and the world.

Closely linked to both the prophetic and priestly task of the Christian family is its kingly role in which it responds to the call to exercise a "service" of love toward God and toward its fellow human beings. Committed to the new commandment of love, the Christian family "welcomes, respects and serves every human being, considering each one in his or her dignity as a person and as a child of God" (FC 63-64). When a husband and wife inspire a love within the family, they promote a personal community which in turn should be extended to both the wider ecclesial community and the world at large. Because of the love in the family, "the Church can and ought to take on a more home life or family dimension developing a more human and fraternal style of relationships" (FC. 63-64).

Thus we find that the family's struggles on its journey of intimacy between husband and wife and parents and children image God and also model a formula for all human relationships. The institutional church can more readily be the "people of God" when it follows the example of a family which is aware of its prophetic, priestly and kingly tasks. Christian families which are struggling with the problems of intimacy in a world of rapidly changing roles can remind the Church of its need to respect the personhood of all its members.

As we indicated previously, angry Catholic women will not be swayed by abstract theological statements. However, the anger of some of these women might be reduced in a family situation where a spouse reveals God as Lover through a commitment to marital intimacy and to the family's participation in the ecclesial task. Family is the "domestic church," a participator in the prophetic, priestly and kingly tasks of Christ in this time and in this place because the Divine Plan for creation made the human sexual attraction a gift for the bonding of two in one flesh, creating a family which would reveal the God in whose image humankind is created. Church leaders, theologians and pastoral ministers who recognize the importance of marital intimacy for the continuation of the original plan of God must challenge families to avoid any role stereotyping that interferes with the bond. At the same time, they should encourage the celebration of both masculinity and femininity in the family. When persons involved in the structure of the institutional church accept the primary importance of the "domestic church" for the formation of the religious imagination, they will have made a step in the right direction toward a positive response to the problems of a modern woman's search for identity.

The significance of the ecclesial task in the life of the Christian family and the role the Christian family plays in the humanization of the larger church have a crucial impact on how the "people of God" image of the Church might make the institutional church more responsive to the personhood of all its members. At the same time, the "domestic church" of individual Christian families needs a continual reminder of its ecclesial task. We must now turn to an investigation of how local religious communities might impact the religious imagination of women while linking the "domestic church" with the wider church community. This linking process offers some hope that the model of the "domestic church" will affect the institutional church, making it more representative of the "people of God" image.

CHAPTER XV: THE PARISH AND DOMESTIC CHURCHES

Thus far in our theological reflections on the sociological investigation of "angry Catholic women" we have argued that a positive theology of sexuality and of marriage would lead to a breakdown in stereotypic expectations for feminine behavior, giving church leaders and pastoral workers a basis for eliminating stereotypic and sexist attitudes towards women. We have also argued that the present clerical-hierarchical structure of the institutional church requires a grass roots elimination of stereotypes, a movement which will help form the "domestic church" as a model for how the institutional manifestation of the "people of God" might alter its style.

However, the "domestic church" of an individual family requires support if it is to endure as "a believing and evangelizing community in dialogue with God and in service to humankind." Indeed, it would be a union of "domestic churches" striving to support women in their search for identity that would forcefully challenge the institutional church to an evaluation of its attitudes and behaviors. Given the diversity of woman's situation in today's world and the toleration in many places for a continuation of stereotypic attitudes toward women, it would seem incumbent upon local churches in those areas where women are consciously struggling in their search for identity to be the places for this grass roots approach to applying a theology of sexuality to the ongoing life of the Church.

Although, as our sociological investigation indicates, less than half the women in America would fall into even the limited sense of "feminism" used in this study, even this percentage makes it impossible for the Church to turn its back on its failure to proclaim a positive theology of sexuality which would recognize the unique personhood of woman. The inability of the Church to respond to the particular problem of "angry Catholic women" stems from its failure to address their need for identity.

While there are women who are not "angry" at the Church for failing to provide them with a vision of sexuality—they continue to attend weekly Mass and even participate in other church activities—this does not mean that these women would not benefit from such a vision. At the present time they are trying to cope with the problems of sexuality and feminine identity assisted only by the secular wisdom which, unfortunately, does not address the Mystery encountered in their search. When women who are confronting the issue of identity in the situation of the family—the "domestic church"—are offered the tools of their faith as a help in resolving this identity, only then will the "domestic churches" be able to model the love necessary for change in the institutional church.

To better understand the process necessary for developing a pastoral theology that will ultimately help the Church address both the concerns of "angry Catholic women" and the broader concerns regarding sexuality and masculinity and femininity in the modern world, we need to consider the interaction between the "domestic church" and the parish. There must be analysis of the importance of pastoral leadership concerned about this issue and of laity willing to press for continual community awareness of the significance of church attention to sexuality and feminine identity.

In the decade since Vatican II the importance of parish has been the subject of much commentary, pro and con. Our sociological investigation of angry Catholic women and our theological reflection in response to this investigation leads us to conclude that at both the theological level and the religious level of religion parish is vitally important. Our theology of sexuality, with its celebration of femininity and its call for marital intimacy, leads inevitably to the realization of the significance of family for both the development of religious imagination and the continuation of religious practices. This conclusion demands a recognition of the need for a link between the "domestic church" of the family and the worldwide institutional church which seeks to publicly continue the prophetic, priestly and kingly task of Jesus Christ. The needs of the "domestic church" and of the worldwide institutional church indicate that a theology of Church is incomplete without a theology of the parish.

We approach the development of a theological vision of parish—a pastoral theology—from the perspective of the "domestic church," realizing that our vision is not the only possible vision of parish but convinced that the reality of the "domestic church" demands that there be some form of local community supportive of the "domestic church" in its fundamental ecclesial tasks. As we consider this theological vision of parish, we will specifically note how this vision might provide a response to the situation of the angry Catholic women. Before outlining our theological vision, we must first respond to some current misconceptions about the relationship of parish and family. There is considerable concern among family life ministers about the possibility that the parish has usurped the religious function of the family. It is not uncommon to hear these ministers talk about the need to "empower" the family, enabling the family to be the religious education center of the child's life. Unfortunately, many of these family life ministers are ignorant of the reality of the "domestic church" which, as we indicated in a previous chapter, is not something set up by a family ministry program, but a fact of family life. The family, consciously or unconsciously, is the first religious educator of the child by virtue of the fact that it socializes the child to values, attitudes and behaviors, preparing the way for religious experience. Family ministry might help develop an awareness of this function of family life, assisting parents in the establishment of an environment which will encourage positive religious experiences, but family ministry does not create the initial empowerment.

So, too, family ministers' concerns about the parish as a detriment to the family's role as religious educator seems to ignore the social phenomenon of community. Human beings are social animals. We do not exist as isolated individuals or as isolated nuclear families. We tend to join with others who share a common perspective and, in the instance of religion, we seek out others who have a common religious perspective as a support for the values and attitudes and behaviors which we find in our faith experience.

Professor McCready has pointed out that just as families socialize their members into attitudes, values and behaviors, parishes (which in the large urban areas of the American church have been synonymous with neighborhood) socialized families into values, attitudes and behaviors which are linked with some common vision of the meaning of life. By offering educational programs and also by exposing the family members to other families who share similar attitudes and values, a parish reinforces the values and attitudes developed in the home. This socialization is both a socialization of the next generation to the values of a religious tradition and a socialization of adult members to attitudes and behaviors helpful for coping with the various crises of adult life.

Our theology of sexuality recognizes that the basic fact of human existence is the creation of humankind, male and female, in the image of God. The powerful physical attraction of woman for man and man for woman offers the possibility of a bonding relationship of marital intimacy, forming a family which continues to proclaim the graciousness of the God who created and redeemed us and continues to grace us in the experience of family life.

Relationships in the family and issues of family life continually confront family members with a sense of Mystery. Family members have the opportunity to discover and reveal God in this encounter with Mystery. But family life also has a potential for demonic and destructive impact on its members. The inevitable joys and sorrows of family experiences require a constant clarification and interpretation through reference to the meaning of life we find in our faith tradition.

We need to be able to speak about the interpretation we give to these experiences and to have our interpretations affirmed by others who have the same religious beliefs. We need to celebrate the God we find in the midst of our family both within the family and within a larger community which shares our sense of joy in the God we experience. The sacramental system affirms the link between the key events of family life and our religious tradition. When we celebrate these events in communion with others, we experience a sharing of common values which affirms our joy in the God who is the source of that joy. The parish community offers the individual "domestic church" the opportunity to experience a sense of affirmation of its ecclesial life.

At the same time, a parish community, at least one modeled after the parish/neighborhood community of the large urban and suburban areas in the United States, is a support community for a family seeking to apply the beliefs of faith to the ongoing joys and sorrows of family experience. Parishes that are successful are ones which challenge and support family members in the crises of family life and encourage them to celebrate the joys of the family.

In addition, the sense of community which exists in a parish/neighborhood offers the opportunity for family members to interact with others who have similar experiences in a context which implies that religion has something to offer to the understanding of those experiences. Women's and men's organizations, teen clubs, home/school organizations, senior citizens clubs, C.F.M., young adult groups, cub scouts, girl scouts, choirs and other parish organizations bring together people of similar interests in an environment which generally leads to a sharing of concerns about family life. Since we all are strongly influenced by our family of birth, even those who are not currently living in a family situation still find the impact of their family experiences either a help or an obstacle in their ability to enter into relationships which will allow us to affirm the goodness of life. Thus it seems safe to assume that everyone in a parish community has a strong need for a community affirmation and celebration of family experiences which reveal the God who

135

created us in such a way that the family is the primary place for our encounter with grace.

A theological vision of parish developed in response to an investigation of the suburban woman and her changing role in the church saw the parish as "the Spirit-filled community which knows of God's plan of salvation through Jesus Christ and proclaims this in celebration and fellowship."[1] This vision sought to articulate the theological dimension of the actual religious experience of the parish and is a basis for a vision of parish which grows out of our understanding of the ecclesial task of the domestic church. Our investigation of family leads us to expand this definition, calling the parish the Spirit-filled community of persons who know the plan of salvation of the God they encounter in family life and relationships through the redemption of Jesus Christ and who proclaim this knowledge in celebration and fellowship. This vision acknowledges the importance of family for the development of religious imagination and challenges pastoral leadership to recognize the primary influence of family and to call upon family members to discover the God present in their everyday experiences. If our premise thus far is correct, if there is a positive theology of sexuality, confirmed by our Catholic Christian tradition, which speaks to modern woman's search for identity and if this theology calls for a transformation of values, attitudes and behaviors regarding women, beginning in the practices of individual families, then it seems that the parish is the context in which family is both challenged and supported in its approach to women. The parish, as the place where a community of "domestic churches" joins to affirm common faith and be nourished by that common faith, must also challenge its members to examine the implications of the common faith for crucial areas of life experience.

It is quite possible that a loving, supportive community with pastoral leadership that encourages it to address the issues of sexuality could counteract the negative image of Church acquired by an alienated Catholic in her youth and reinforced by activity within the wider institutional church. At the same time, once a sufficient number of parish communities begin seriously to address the issue of sexuality and its implications for women's role, they should be able to articulate out of their experiences a pastoral theology which could challenge the institutional church to "develop a more human and fraternal style of relationship."

Parishes are engaged in giving rather mixed signals on woman's role in the church. Certainly women appear to be much more active than they were in previous generations. Today, women are presidents of parish councils; serve on liturgy committees; teach C.C.D.; are lectors, commentators and ministers of communion; have replaced the teaching sisters in the parochial schools; are directors of religious education, ministers of care and, at times, even pastoral associates. The modern, thriving, urban or suburban parish could not survive without the services, both professional and volunteer, of large numbers of women.

Still, we suspect that close examination of the majority of parishes would reveal that few of these women are regarded as religious leaders of the parishes in which they live and work. What women are doing in parishes today is most often the equivalent of the serving role they played in the large urban parishes prior to the Second Vatican Council. They serve the pastors in the sense that they perform tasks which make it possible for the pastors to exercise religious leadership. Indeed, it is highly possible that women have given up a certain degree of the religious leadership that they held in the past when the religious women teaching in the schools were regarded, at least by the laity, as important influences on religious development.

In addition, few if any parishes give attention to issues of sexuality, marital intimacy, the celebration of femininity or the way in which the family socializes its members into values, attitudes and behaviors regarding the role of women, even though these issues are crucially important if the "domestic church" is to perform its ecclesial tasks. In an earlier work on leadership for the local church, we emphasized the important role the priest leader plays in determining the direction the parish takes on crucial issues. Sociological analysis of the angry Catholic woman also affirms the possibility of a priest suppressing the anger which some women, (given their similarity in other ways to the angry Catholic woman) might have toward the Church. Combining these two investigations of the role of the priest indicates that the pastor of a parish plays a crucial role in the task of forming a Spirit-filled community that recognizes the God its members encounter in their familial experiences. And to the degree that other non-ordained members of the parish staff are viewed as sharing in the leadership role of the pastor, they, too, will influence the ability of a parish community to recognize its role in the search for woman's identity in the modern world.

The religious leader who recognizes the importance of a theology of sexuality, a theology of marital intimacy, the personhood of woman and the influence of the "domestic church" on the religious imagination assists the parish community by helping its members discover the religious dimensions of those experiences which often seem to be only ordinary experiences. The pastor (and all pastoral leadership) is the faith reflector in the parish community, the one who identifies the presence of God in people and the presence of people in God, both in liturgical and nonliturgical activity. The task of pastoral leadership is the correlation of the convictions and values of the Christian faith to the ongoing life of the community, helping the people to uncover the Divine Lure in their midst. The pastor does this best by listening to the articulated and unarticulated concerns of the people and bringing to them the Christian message as a clarifier to these concerns.

In today's world a pastoral listener who is faithfully performing this task cannot help but hear the concerns related to sexuality, women's personhood, marital intimacy and family life. The fact that most parishes do not respond to these concerns would seem to indicate that pastors have not listened carefully enough to the deep and often unarticulated obstacles that a lack of a positive theology of sexuality and its implications for marriage and personhood has created for people in the modern world. Pastors, like everyone else, are subject to the cultural and religious situations which have encouraged stereotypes about marriage, family life and male and female roles, stereotypes which are deeply ingrained and often interfere with a pastor's ability to recognize them as contrary to the beliefs of our faith.

Our theology of sexuality demands a recognition of the personhood of both man and woman, directly requiring that all human relationships, and particularly church centered relationships, be based on a recognition of

the personhood of the people involved. This theology places a heavy bur-
den on pastors. They must seek to eliminate their own stereotypic values,
attitudes and behaviors if they wish to be faith reflectors in this critical area of the lives of their people.

At the same time that we acknowledge the central role of the pastoral
leader in eliminating the negative image of the Church as supporter of stereotypes for women, we must also recognize the responsibility of the laity
in this area. While in most instances the pastoral leader creates the environment of the parish community, the laity, by its willingness to abdicate total responsibility for the correlations of life and faith to the
pastor, often fails in its responsibility to continue the task of the
Kingdom of God. With increased education, the laity is often in a better
position than the pastor to identify certain issues of concern in the parish community and bears a responsibility for asking for
religious clarification of the dilemmas encountered in many of these
experiences.

In our Catholic communities, where the principal pastoral leader is a
celibate male, it is possible that the concerns we have addressed in our
reflections are not as apparent to the pastor as they would be to lay members of the community. When that is the case, then the laity has the
right and the duty to call for pastoral response to the sense of confusion
and mystery encountered in these experiences. The "domestic church" cannot perform its prophetic, priestly and kingly role in the modern world
without a continuing, clarifying faith perspective on the critical issues
of family life.

Those extraordinary experiences which offer the potential for the revelation of God and which have been rendered ordinary and potentially
demonic demand that family members have continual reminders of the relationship of faith to these experiences. Angry Catholic women have not
been offered this clarification in their search for an identity in the modern world. They, and other laity, should not be content with the failure
of pastors to address these issues. Though the primary responsibility for
faith reflection resides with the pastor, the laity cannot abdicate the
task of the "domestic church" which requires that they develop a better appreciation of issues of sexuality, marital intimacy and the personhood of
women.

Perhaps, over time, the presence of women active in a variety of different roles within a parish will break down the resistance to women functioning as religious leaders and role models for younger women. Still,
there is a need to see this possibility of religious leadership by women
as part of the larger task of developing an appreciation in the parish
community for a theology of sexuality, a theology which affirms the
support of the religious tradition for women's contribution to religious
leadership.

If the parish embraces a theology of sexuality such as the one we
have proposed, it will, of necessity, be forced to deal with the issue of
role stereotypes in the "domestic church," in the parish community, in the
universal church and in society. Discussions of these issues would in
turn lead to an examination of new roles in the family and in the parish
community for both men and women. Once a parish-wide "conversation" about
sexuality is seriously begun, sex role stereotypes and new identities for

men and women will inevitably contribute to an interaction between individual "domestic churches" and the broader parish community. The effect of this dialoguing will be an increase in the ability of the Christian family and of the Church to influence attitudes on women's place in our society.

Though we do not propose specific programs for parishes seeking to respond to the "angry Catholic women" in their midst, we are suggesting, in our theological reflections on the sociological investigation of these women, that the most fruitful sphere of action for responding to these women is the local parish. Here interaction between "domestic church" and parish community could develop a grass roots pastoral theology where the interaction of a common faith experience with the mystery of human sexuality leads to an articulation of values and attitudes and behaviors concerning sexuality, sex roles, marriage and the family. If a sufficient number of parish churches would undertake such an enterprise, "angry Catholic women" might be more apt to experience a positive encounter with a Church supportive of women's search for identity. If parishes do not begin to address these issues, then for the foreseeable future, a percentage of women will continue to experience the Church as hostile to women's search for identity. At the parish level, both pastoral leaders and concerned laity should be about the task of examining how they are responding to a critical challenge made most obvious in our analysis of "angry Catholic women."

AFTERWORD

By Andrew M. Greeley

In the summer of 1983, as this volume was being readied for the publisher, two incidents occurred which neatly illustrated the problems involved in any attempt by the Catholic Church to respond to its alienated women members -- the dismissal from the religious life of Sister Mary Mancour by the Archbishop of Detroit and the ban on women servers at Mass by the Cardinal Archbishop of Chicago.

It is beyond the scope of this book to comment directly on either case. One need only observe that in a Church in which the leadership was aware of the magnitude of the problem of women's alienation neither crisis would have been permitted to happen. The Archbishop of Detroit felt free to force a nun out of the religious life to reassert his power and authority and the Cardinal Archbishop of Chicago was astonished by the vehemence of the reaction of his routine letter on "altar girls" because church leadership is monumentally insensitive to the dimensions of its "women problem."

One member of the chancery staff in Chicago told a woman on a committee protesting the altar girl ban that the majority of Catholic women in Chicago did not agree with her. It is to be wondered how he knew. Surely there is no empirical evidence to support his argument nor is there any inclination to seek the empirical evidence. The non-existence of a women problem is not an empirical conclusion but an <u>a priori</u> act of faith with much of the clergy and most of the hierarchy. As a matter of definition, "feminism" is limited only to a few nuns who want to be ordained and a few outspoken supporters of ERA and/or abortion. The good Catholic wife and mother of myth and fable is presumed to be as loyal as she always was to ecclesiastical authority.

Such a mentality precludes the possibility of church authority responding to the problem we have outlined in this report. And the Detroit and Chicago scandals of the summer of '83 reveal how simple-minded the mentality is.

Probably neither case caused many women to discontinue church attendance. As we have explained in this book, it is past history rather than present reality which accounts for "anger" (as we have defined it). Doubtless the Mancour case and the altar girl ban have made a lot of Catholic women angry in the ordinary sense of that word. But as we have also tried to explain that anger does not turn people away from the Church; it rather makes them even more furious participants.

It is not that church authorities do not care about the anger, in either sense of the word; rather, they simply do not see it because they refuse to admit its possibility. The data in the present report must be rejected out of hand because it does not fit the unassailable paradigms of the ecclesiastical mind.

Hence there is no need to take seriously the positive pastoral suggestions presented in the constructive part of our study. The typical bishop and the typical pastor might agree that the recommendations are interesting and indeed would be very useful if the Church had a massive "women problem." But since it does not, then the recommendations can safely be ignored. It is a fairly melancholy conclusion, but one which at the present time is inescapable. Church leadership does not see a women problem because it does not want to, perhaps because it is afraid to.

It is the response of men on a low lying coast with storm warnings posted for all to see and the eye of the hurricane rushing towards them, who still insist that it is not even raining.

FOOTNOTES

Chapter 9

[1] The papal addresses are recorded in <u>L'Osservatore Romano</u> beginning in September, 1979 and continuing through the time of this writing (March, 1983). For a pastoral analysis of the first fifty-six addresses see: <u>A Feast of Love: Pope John Paul on Human Intimacy</u>, Mary G. Durkin, Chicago: Loyola University Press, 1983.

Chapter 10

[1] For example, see: Leonard Swidler, <u>Biblical Affirmations of Women</u>, Philadelphia: The Westminster Press, 1979.

[2] Kathryn Allen Rabuzzi, <u>The Sacred and the Feminine: Toward a Theology of Housework</u>, New York: The Seabury Press, 1982.

Chapter 11

[1] Eileen Zieget Silbermann, <u>The Savage Sacrament: A Theology of Marriage After American Feminism</u>, Mystic, Connecticut: Twenty-Third Publications, 1983.

[2] For a more detailed analysis of the pastoral theology developed in this symposium see: Joan Meyer Anzia and Mary G. Durkin, <u>Marital Intimacy: A Catholic Perspective</u>, Chicago: Loyola U. Press, 1982.

Chapter 13

[1] Mary G. Durkin, <u>The Suburban Woman: Her Changing Role in the Church</u>, New York: The Seabury Press, 1974.

TABLES

148

TABLE 1.1

SUPPORT FOR ORDINATION OF WOMEN AND WORKING MOTHERS BY SEX
(For Catholics between 18 and 30)

	Men	Women
Ordination[1]	42%	47%
Working Mothers[2]	58%	56%
Support both	25%	33%

[1]How important..."Allow women to become priests..." Percent extremely or somewhat important.

[2]A preschool child is "likely to suffer emotional damage if the Mother works..." Percent disagree strongly or disagree somewhat.

149

TABLE 1.2

CHURCH ATTENDANCE FOR WOMEN BY "FEMINIST" ATTITUDES

Percent Regular[3] Church

	Percent
"Feminists"[4]	30
Not "Feminists"	47

[3]Attend at least two or three times a month.

[4]Extremely important or somewhat important that women be ordained AND disagree strongly or somewhat that preschool child will suffer emotional damage.

150

TABLE 1.2A

ATTITUDES AND BEHAVIOR OF "FEMINISTS" AND NOT "FEMINISTS"
(Women only)

	"Feminists"	Not "Feminists"
Approval of abortion if risk to mother	89%	81%
If mother wants no more children	62%*	38%
Approve of living together before marriage	60%*	42%
Sermons excellent or good	44%	45%
Priests are "understanding"	33%	35%
Priests expect laity to be followers	54%	58%
Priests are only interested in selves	20%	20%
Would object to a daughter as a nun	42%	31%
Single	43%	37%
Happy childhood	38%	34%
Number of children expected	2.1	2.5*
Happily married	62%	64%
Sexual fulfillment in marriage excellent	50%	45%

*Significant difference between "Feminists" and Not "Feminists."

TABLE 1.3

CHURCH ATTENDANCE FOR WOMEN BY "FEMINIST" ATTITUDES
BY CONFIDENCE IN CHURCH LEADERS[5]

	"Feminists"	Not "Feminists"
A great deal of confidence	60%	67%
Not a great deal of confidence	22%	38%*

*Significantly different from "Feminists."

[5]How much confidence do you have in the people...running
organized religion. Percent "a great deal of confidence."

TABLE 1.4

CHURCH ATTENDANCE FOR WOMEN BY "FEMINIST" ATTITUDES
BY COLLEGE ATTENDANCE
(Percent regular church attenders)

	"Feminists"	Not "Feminists"
Attended college	26	49*
Did not attend college	36	44

*Significantly different from "Feminists."

TABLE 1.5

CHURCH ATTENDANCE FOR WOMEN BY "FEMINIST" ATTITUDES BY CONFIDENCE
IN CHURCH LEADERSHIP BY COLLEGE ATTENDANCE
(Percent not confident only)

	"Feminists"	Not "Feminists"
Attended college	20	40*
Did not attend college	24	34

*Significantly different from "Feminists."

TABLE 1.6

EXPLANATION OF DIFFERENCE IN CHURCH ATTENDANCE
BETWEEN "FEMINISTS" AND NOT "FEMINISTS"

Raw difference	17%
Net of confidence in church leaders	13%
Net of interaction between "Feminism" and education	12%
Net of interaction between education and confidence	05%**

**Difference not statistically significant.

TABLE 2.1

MASS ATTENDANCE FOR CATHOLIC "FEMINISTS" BY WHETHER MOTHERS WORKED
WHEN THEY WERE PRESCHOOL CHILDREN
College Attenders Only
(Percent Regular Attendance)

	Mother Worked	
	Yes	No
"Feminists"	34 (32)	19 (57)
Not "Feminists"	45 (35)	49* (100)

* Significant difference from "Feminists."

156

TABLE 2.2

MASS ATTENDANCE FOR CATHOLIC "FEMINISTS" WHO ARE NOT CONFIDENT IN
CHURCH LEADERS AND WHO WENT TO COLLEGE BY WHETHER
THEIR MOTHERS WORKED WHEN THEY WERE UNDER SIX
(Percent low confidence only)

	"Feminists"	Not "Feminists"
Mothers did work	37 (26)	31 (28)
Mothers did not work	16 (45)	47* (74)

*Significantly different from "Feminists."

TABLE 2.3

EXPLANATION OF DIFFERENCE IN CHURCH DEVOTION FOR CATHOLIC WOMEN
WHO WENT TO COLLEGE WHO ARE "FEMINISTS" AND NOT "FEMINISTS"

Raw difference between "Feminists" and not "Feminists"	23%
Interaction between Mother's work and "Feminism"	-03%
Interaction between "Feminism" and confidence in church leadership	+10%

TABLE 3.1

MASS ATTENDANCE OF CATHOLIC "FEMINISTS" WHO WENT TO COLLEGE AND
WHOSE MOTHERS DID NOT WORK BY THEIR MOTHERS' MASS ATTENDANCE
(Percent regular Church attenders)

	"Feminists"	Not "Feminists"
Mother attended every week	19	56*
	(37)	(64)
Mother attended less than every week	16	36
	(15)	(36)

*Significantly different from "Feminists."

TABLE 3.2

MASS ATTENDANCE OF CATHOLIC "FEMINISTS" WHO WENT TO COLLEGE AND
WHOSE MOTHERS DID NOT WORK AND WHOSE MOTHERS ATTENDED MASS EVERY WEEK
BY WHETHER RESPONDENT FEELS CLOSE TO GOD

	"Feminists"	Not "Feminists"
Feels extremely close to God or very close	33% (15)	61% (30)
Less than very close	10% (20)	50%* (23)

*Significantly different from "Feminists."

TABLE 3.3

EXPLANATION OF DIFFERENCES BETWEEN "FEMINISTS" AND
NOT "FEMINISTS" IN MASS ATTENDANCE

	Percent
Raw difference between "Feminists" and not "Feminists"	30
Confidence in Church leadership	26
Mother's Mass attendance	20
Interaction between "Feminism" and Mother's Mass attendance	16
Interaction between "Feminism" and closeness to God	5**

**Difference not statistically significant.

TABLE 3.4

SPECIFICATION OF DIFFERENCE IN MASS ATTENDANCE
BETWEEN "FEMINISTS" AND NOT "FEMINISTS"
(Difference in regular attendance
between "Feminists" and not "Feminists")

	Percent
All	12
Women	17
College educated women	22
College educated women whose mothers did not work while they were infants	30
College educated women whose mothers did not work but were devout church-goers	37
College educated women whose devout mothers did not work and who do not feel close to God	40

TABLE 3.4A

MASS ATTENDANCE FOR CATHOLIC "FEMINISTS" BY WHETHER MOTHER WORKED
BEFORE THE RESPONDENT WAS SIX YEARS OLD
(Percent Regular Church Attendance)

Mother worked	37% (48)
Mother did not work	25% (99)

TABLE 3.5

MASS ATTENDANCE FOR CATHOLIC "FEMINISTS" BY WHETHER MOTHER WORKED
BEFORE THE RESPONDENT WAS SIX YEARS OLD BY IMAGE OF GOD AS "LOVER"
(Percent Regular Church Attendance)

	Mother worked	Mother did not work
"Extremely likely" to imagine God as a "Lover"	69* (25)	27 (22)
Less than "extremely likely"	25 (35)	24 (77)

*Significantly different from those less likely
to imagine God as "Lover."

TABLE 3.6

MASS ATTENDANCE FOR CATHOLIC "FEMINISTS" BY MOTHER'S MASS ATTENDANCE
(Percent Regular Church Attendance)

Mother went to weekly Mass	32% (99)
Mother did not go to weekly Mass	29% (31)

TABLE 3.7

MASS ATTENDANCE FOR CATHOLIC "FEMINISTS" BY MOTHER'S MASS ATTENDANCE
AND IMAGE OF GOD AS "LOVER"
(Percent Regular Church Attendance)

	Mother went to Mass weekly	Mother did not go to Mass weekly
"Extremely likely" to imagine God as "Lover"	35% (20)	60% (10)*
Less than "extremely likely" to imagine God as "Lover"	31% (79)	14% (21)

*Significantly different from those less than "extremely likely" to imagine God as "Lover."

164

TABLES FROM NORC GENERAL SOCIAL SURVEY (GENSOC)

TABLE 4.1

"FEMINISM" BY SEX BY YEAR
(Percentage "Feminist")

	Men	Women
1974-75	38	41
1977-78	39	43
1982	41	57*
All	39	44

* Significantly different from Men.

TABLE 4.2

"FEMINISM" BY SEX BY AGE

	Men	Women
20's and younger	49	59
30's	37	54
40's	35	42
50's and over	33	22

TABLE 4.3

CHURCH ATTENDANCE BY "FEMINISM"
(Percent Weekly)

	"Feminists"	Not "Feminists"
Men	39	40
Women	40	54

TABLE 4.4

CHURCH ATTENDANCE BY "FEMINISM" BY AGE AND EDUCATION
(Women Only)

	"Feminists"	Not "Feminists"
College (18-30)	34% (64)	70%* (30)
Not College (18-30)	26% (81)	36% (71)
College (over 30)	63% (71)	76% (43)
Not College (over 30)	52% (115)	61% (281)

* Difference is statistically significant.

166

TABLE 4.5

CHURCH ATTENDANCE BY "FEMINISM" BY AGE, EDUCATION
AND MOTHER'S WORK WHEN CHILD
FOR WOMEN ONLY--AGE 18-30
(Respondent attended college only)

	"Feminists"	Not "Feminists"
Mother worked before child was six	39%	39%
Mother did not work	37%	56%*

* Difference is statistically significant.

TABLE 4.6

CHURCH ATTENDANCE BY "FEMINISM" BY CONFIDENCE IN THE CLERGY
FOR WOMEN ONLY
(Percent regular church attendance)

	"Feminists"	Not "Feminists"
Very Confident	36	52*
Not Very Confident	62	69

* Difference is statistically significant.

TABLE 4.7

CHURCH ATTENDANCE BY "FEMINISM" BY HOUSEWIFE

	"Feminists"	Not "Feminists"
Housewife – Yes	45	63*
Housewife – No	42	50

* Difference is statistically significant.

TABLE 4.8

CHURCH ATTENDANCE BY "FEMINISM" BY HAPPINESS IN MARRIAGE

	"Feminists"	Not "Feminists"
Very Happy	50	67*
Less than Very Happy	36	51*

* Difference is statistically significant.

TABLE 4.9

CHURCH ATTENDANCE BY "FEMINISM" BY FAMILY SATISFACTION

	"Feminists"	Not "Feminists"
Very Satisfied	50%	58%
Less than Very Satisfied	40%	60%[*]

* Difference is statistically significant.

TABLE 4.10

CHURCH ATTENDANCE BY "FEMINISM" BY FAMILY SATISFACTION BY HOUSEWIFE
(for housewife only)

	"Feminists"	Not "Feminists"
Very Satisfied	51%	59%
Less than Very Satisfied	42%	65%[*]

* Difference is statistically significant.

TABLE 4.11

CHURCH ATTENDANCE BY "FEMINISM" BY FAMILY SATISFACTION
BY HOUSEWIVES BY CONFIDENCE IN THE CLERGY
(for housewives with low family satisfaction only)

	"Feminists"	Not "Feminists"
Very Confident in Leadership	66%	72%
Less than Very Confident in Leadership	33%	62%[*]

* Difference is statistically significant.

TABLE 4.12

CHURCH ATTENDANCE BY "FEMINISM" BY WHETHER MOTHER WORKED
WHEN CHILD WAS UNDER SIX

	"Feminists"	Not "Feminists"
Mother worked	43%	47%
Mother did not work	41%	59%[*]

* Difference is statistically significant.

170

TABLE 4.13

CHURCH ATTENDANCE BY "FEMINISM" BY WHETHER MOTHER WORKED
WHEN CHILD WAS UNDER SIX
FOR DISSATISFIED HOUSEWIVES ONLY

	"Feminists"	Not "Feminists"
Mother worked	30%	61%
Mother did not work	28%	68%*

*Difference is statistically significant.

TABLE 4.14

EXPLANATION OF DIFFERENCE IN CHURCH ATTENDANCE
BETWEEN "FEMINISTS" AND NOT "FEMINISTS"

Raw Difference	14%
Interaction Between "Feminism" and Family Satisfaction	05%
Interaction between "Feminism" and Confidence in Church Leadership	0%

TABLE 5.1
"FEMINISM" BY SEX BY DENOMINATION
(Percent "Feminist")
(General Social Survey)

	Men	Women
Catholics	39	44
Baptists	29	32
Methodists	35	36
Lutheran	45	38
Presbyterian	45	46
Episcopalian	61	50
Other Protestants	33	34
No Denomination	43	46
Jews	56	66

TABLE 5.2

CHURCH ATTENDANCE BY "FEMINISM" BY DENOMINATION - WOMEN ONLY
(Percent Regular Church Attendance)
(General Social Survey)

	"Feminists"	Not "Feminists"
Baptist	27	47*
Methodist	33	37
Lutheran	30	38
Presbyterian	26	39

* Significant difference from "Feminists."

TABLE 5.3

CHURCH ATTENDANCE BY "FEMINISM" BY CONFIDENCE
IN CHURCH LEADERSHIP FOR BAPTISTS

	"Feminists"	Not "Feminists"
Very Confident	41%	50%
Less than Very Confident	23%	44%*

* Significant difference from "Feminists."

TABLE 5.4

"FEMINISM" BY POLITICAL AND IDEOLOGICAL SELF-IDENTIFICATION (GENSOC)
(Percent "Feminists")

	Liberal	Moderate	Conservative
Democratic	47%	35%	40%
Independent	61%	45%	55%
Republican	43%	38%	48%

TABLE 5.5

RELATIONSHIP BETWEEN "FEMINISM" AND CHURCH ATTENDANCE
BY POLITICAL AND IDEOLOGICAL SELF-DESCRIPTION (GENSOC)
(r)

	Liberal	Moderate	Conservative
Democratic	.22*	.20*	.07
Independent	.32*	.02	.09
Republican	.71*	.00	.25

* Significant relationships. (Since two-by-two tables are being used, these numbers also represent percentage point differences.)

174

TABLE 6.2

"FEMINISM" BY SEX AND CULTURE FOR CATHOLICS BETWEEN 18 AND 31

	Men	Women
English-Canadian	34%	52%*
Anglo-American[1]	26%	34%*
French-Canadian	24%	26%
Hispanic-American	29%	23%

* Significantly different from men.
[1] Non hispanic.

TABLE 6.3

"FEMINISM" AND CHURCH ATTENDANCE BY SEX AND CULTURE FOR WOMEN

	English Canadian	Anglo American	French Canadian	Hispanic American
"Feminists"/Women	27%	29%	31%	36%
Not "Feminists"/Women	54%*	47%*	36%	36% (25)
"Feminists"/Men	20%	23%	12%	0 (10)
Not "Feminists"/Men	24%	31%*	33%*	32% (36)

* Significant difference between "Feminists" and Not "Feminists."

175

TABLE 6.4

MODELS TO EXPLAIN DIFFERENCES IN CHURCH ATTENDANCE
BETWEEN "FEMINISTS" AND NOT "FEMINISTS" FOR ENGLISH
CANADIAN WOMEN AND FRENCH CANADIAN MEN

	English Women	French Men
Raw difference	27	20
Confidence in Church Leadership	27	19
Interaction with Education	15	18
Interaction with Confidence in Church Leadership	14*	18

* Significant reduction of raw difference.

TABLE 6.5

"FEMINISM" AND CHURCH ATTENDANCE FOR
AMERICAN MEN BY COLLEGE EDUCATION
(Percent regular church attendance)

	"Feminists"	Not "Feminists"
Attended College	17%	30%*
Did Not Attend College	26%	31%

* Significantly different from "Feminists."

TABLE 6.6

"FEMINISM" AND CHURCH ATTENDANCE FOR AMERICANS WITH
COLLEGE EDUCATION BY WHETHER THEIR MOTHERS
WORKED WHEN THEY WERE LESS THAN SIX YEARS OLD

	"Feminists"	Not "Feminists"
Mother worked	11%	23%
Mother did not work	17%	35%*

* Significantly different from "Feminists."

TABLE 7.1

CORRELATES BETWEEN A WOMAN'S "FEMINISM"
AND THAT OF HER HUSBAND

All Women	.18
Women 18-25	.33
Women 26-30	.07

178

TABLE 7.2

EXPECTED AND ACTUAL "FEMINISM" OF HUSBAND
BY AGE OF WIFE

	18-25	26-30
Expected	39%	24%
Actual	62%	29%
Ratio	1.6	1.2

TABLE 7.3

FAMILY RELATIONSHIPS BY "FEMINISM" OF WIFE

	Marital Satisfaction of both husband and wife (% both very satisfied)	Sexual Fulfillment of both (% excellent)
Wife "Feminist"	55%	26%
Wife not "Feminist"	51%	28%

TABLE 7.4

FAMILY RELATIONSHIPS BY "FEMINISM" OF HUSBAND

	Marital Satisfaction	Sexual Fulfillment
Husband "Feminist"	63%	37%*
Husband not "Feminist"	49%*	23%

*Statistically Significant difference from not "Feminists."

181

TABLE 7.5

FAMILY RELATIONSHIPS AND WIFE'S "FEMINISM" BY AGE

	Marital Satisfaction	Sexual Fulfillment
Wife is 18-25		
"Feminist"	67%*	42%*
Not "Feminist"	51%	22%
Wife is 26-30		
"Feminist"	56%	30%
Not "Feminist"	45%	30%

* Statistically significant difference from not "Feminists."

TABLE 7.6

FAMILY RELATIONSHIPS BY "FEMINISM" OF HUSBAND
AND AGE OF WIFE

	Marital Satisfaction	Sexual Fulfillment
Wife is 18-25		
"Feminist" Husband	64%	42%*
Not "Feminist"	66%	23%
Wife is 26-30		
"Feminist" Husband	59%	22%
Not "Feminist"	51%	22%

*Statistically significant difference from not "Feminists."

TABLE 7.7

CHURCH ATTENDANCE OF WOMAN BY "FEMINISM" OF WOMAN
AND CHURCH ATTENDANCE OF HER HUSBAND
(Percent Wife "Regular")

	Husband "regular"	Husband not "regular"
"Feminist"	74%	5%
Not "Feminist"	66%	22%*

*Statistically significant difference from "Feminist."

TABLE 7.8

CHURCH ATTENDANCE OF HUSBAND BY "FEMINISM" OF WIFE
(Percent husbands attend regularly)

"Feminist"	29%
Not "Feminist"	39%*

*Statistically significant difference from "Feminist."

TABLE 7.9

CHURCH ATTENDANCE OF HUSBAND BY WHETHER WIFE'S MOTHER
WORKED BEFORE SHE WAS SIX
(Percent husbands attend regularly)

	Mother worked	Mother did not work
"Feminist	38%	24%
Not "Feminist"	38%	44%*

*Statistically significant difference from "Feminist."

TABLE 7.10

HUSBAND'S CHURCH ATTENDANCE BY AGE OF WIFE
AND WIFE'S "FEMINISM"
(Percent husbands attend regularly)

	18-25	26-30
"Feminist"	39%	23%
Not "Feminist"	21%	43%*

*Statistically significant difference from "Feminist."

TABLE 7.11

CHURCH ATTENDANCE OF YOUNG WOMEN BY WHETHER THEY PERCEIVE
HUSBAND AS A RELIGIOUS INFLUENCE BY WIFE'S "FEMINISM"
(Percent wife regular attendance)

| | Husband's influence | |
	"Very great"	Not "very great"
"Feminist"	57%	18%
Not "Feminist"	61%	38%*

*Statistically significant difference from "Feminist."

188

TABLE 7.12

CHURCH ATTENDANCE OF YOUNG WOMEN BY WHETHER THEY PERCEIVE
MOTHER AS A RELIGIOUS INFLUENCE BY THEIR OWN "FEMINISM"

| | Mother's influence | |
	"Very great"	Not "very great"
"Feminist"	44%	22%
Not "Feminist"	57%*	37%*

*Statistically significant difference from "Feminist."

TABLE 7.13

IMAGE OF GOD AS "LOVER" BY HUSBAND'S "FEMINISM"
(Percent of women "extremely likely"
to imagine God as "Lover")

	"Feminist" Women	Not "Feminist" Women
"Feminist" husband	36%*	23%
Not "Feminist" husband	24%	28%

"Statistically different from all others.

TABLE 8.1

ATTITUDES OF "FEMINISTS" TOWARDS CLERGY

	"Feminists"	Not "Feminists"
Priests in Parish are very sympathetic	31%	34%
Serious talk with Priest during past year	15%	15%
Priest had "very much" affect on religious feeling	16%	18%

TABLE 8.2

CHURCH ATTENDANCE OF "FEMINISTS"
BY EMPATHY OF PARISH PRIESTS

	"Feminists"	Not "Feminists"
Priests "very" sympathetic	64%	67%
Priests less than "very" sympathetic	43%	56%*

*Significantly different from "Feminists."

TABLE 8.3

CHURCH ATTENDANCE BY INFLUENCE OF PRIEST
(Percent Regular Church Attendance)

	"Feminists"	Not "Feminists"
Priest "influential"*	75%	78%
Priest not "influential"	27%	42%**

* Has talked to a priest in the last year and feels that a priest has had a great influence on her religious attitudes.

** Significant difference from "Feminists."

TABLE 8.4

CORRELATIONS BETWEEN IMAGE OF GOD AS "LOVER"
AND INFLUENCE OF PRIESTS
FOR "FEMINISTS" AND NOT "FEMINISTS"

	"Feminists"	Not "Feminists"
Sympathy	.18*	.02
Influence	.22*	.13

* Significant correlation.

TABLE 8.5

MASS ATTENDANCE FOR "FEMINISTS" BY SYMPATHY OF PRIEST
AND IMAGE OF GOD AS "LOVER"
(Percent Regular Mass Attendance)

	"Feminists"	Not "Feminists"
Priests "Very Understanding"		
"Extremely likely" to imagine God as "Lover"	90%	72%
Less than "extremely likely"	50%	65%
Priests not "Very Understanding"		
"Extremely likely"	58%	59%
Less than "extremely likely"	40%	55%*

* Significantly different from "Feminists."

TABLE 8.6

MASS ATTENDANCE FOR "FEMINISTS" BY IMAGE OF GOD
AND INFLUENCE OF PRIEST
(Percent Regular Church Attendance)

	"Feminists"	Not "Feminists"
Priest Influential		
"Extremely likely" to imagine God as "Lover"	83%	75%
Not "extremely likely"	67%	75%
Priest not Influential		
"Extremely likely"	40%	53%
Not "extremely likely"	23%	40%*

* Statistically significant difference from "Feminists."

TABLE 8.7

SYMPATHY OF PRIESTS BY WHETHER RESPONDENT
HAS HAD SERIOUS TALK WITH PRIEST BY "FEMINISM"
(Percent of Priests "Very Understanding")

	"Feminist"	Not "Feminist"
Talked with priest in past year	47%	43%
Has not talked with priest	27%*	32%

* Significantly different from those "Feminists" who have not talked to priest.

TABLE 8.8

"RETURN TO CHURCH" BY CONVERSATION WITH PRIEST FOR "FEMINISTS"
(Percent closer to church than they were five years ago)

	"Feminists"	Not "Feminists"
Talked with priest	32%	33%
Did not talk with priest	15%*	20%*

* Significantly different from those who did not talk to priests.

198

TABLE 8.9

"RETURN TO CHURCH" BY SYMPATHY OF PARISH PRIESTS
(Percent closer to Church than they were five years ago)

	"Feminists"	Not "Feminists"
Priest "very understanding"	47%	33%
Priest less than "very understanding"	23%*	28%

* Significantly different from those who think their parish priests
are "very understanding."

TABLE 8.10

"RETURN TO CHURCH" FOR "FEMINISTS"
BY CONVERSATION WITH A PRIEST
AND SYMPATHY OF PARISH PRIESTS
(Percent closer to Church than five years ago)

	"Feminists"	Not "Feminists"
Priest "Very Understanding"		
Had conversation	60%	24%
Did not have conversation	50%	28%
Priest not "Very Understanding"		
Had conversation	18%	45%*
Did not have conversation	20%	28%

* Significantly different from those who did not have conversation.

FIGURES

NOW   CHILDHOOD

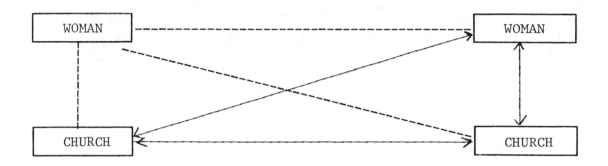

——— Positive

----- Negative

FIGURE 2.1

IMAGE CONFLICT FOR CATHOLIC FEMINISTS

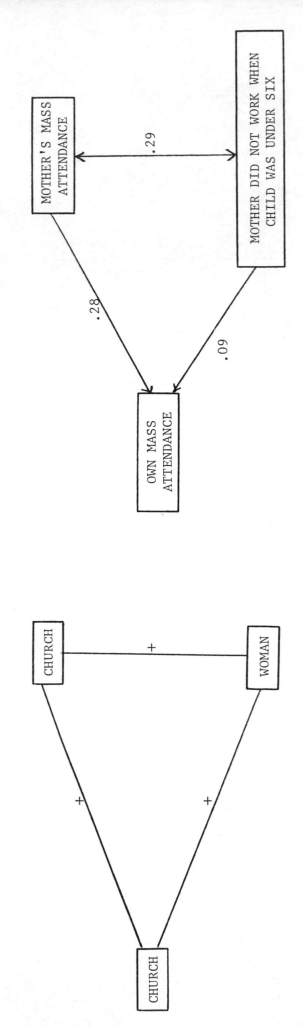

A) HYPOTHESIZED RELATIONSHIPS

B) ACTUAL RELATIONSHIPS

FIGURE 2.2

RELATIONSHIP AMONG IMAGES FOR "TRADITIONAL" WOMEN

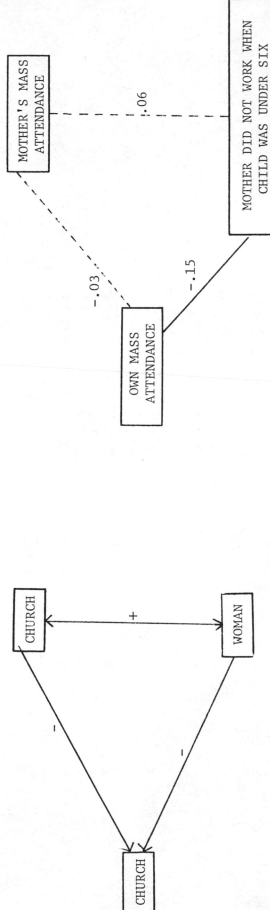

B) ACTUAL

MOTHER'S MASS ATTENDANCE

-.06

MOTHER DID NOT WORK WHEN CHILD WAS UNDER SIX

-.03

-.15

OWN MASS ATTENDANCE

A) HYPOTHETICAL

CHURCH

+

WOMAN

-

-

CHURCH

FIGURE 2.3

RELATIONSHIP AMONG IMAGES FOR "FEMINIST" WOMEN

NOW   CHILDHOOD

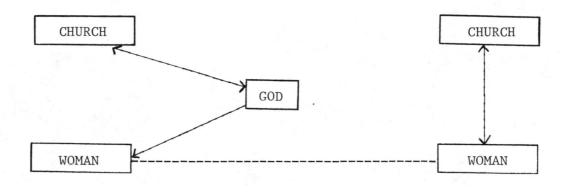

```
—————  Positive
— — —  Negative
```

FIGURE 3.1

IMAGE OF GOD AS SUPPRESSOR OF IMAGE CONFLICT FOR CATHOLIC FEMINISTS

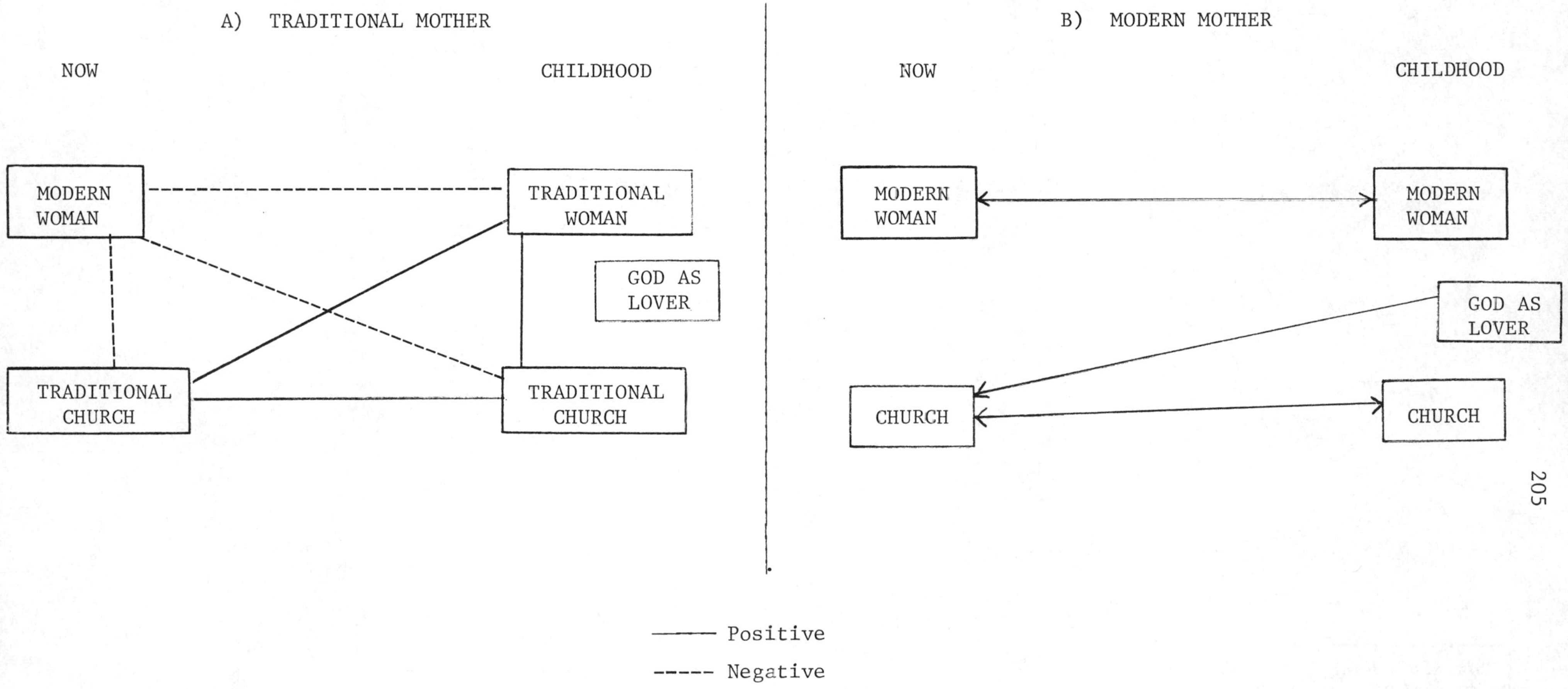

A) TRADITIONAL MOTHER

NOW   CHILDHOOD

MODERN WOMAN

TRADITIONAL WOMAN

GOD AS LOVER

TRADITIONAL CHURCH

TRADITIONAL CHURCH

B) MODERN MOTHER

NOW   CHILDHOOD

MODERN WOMAN

MODERN WOMAN

GOD AS LOVER

CHURCH

CHURCH

——— Positive

- - - - - Negative

FIGURE 3.2

INFLUENCE OF NON-TRADITIONAL IMAGE OF GOD ON IMAGE OF CHURCH

206

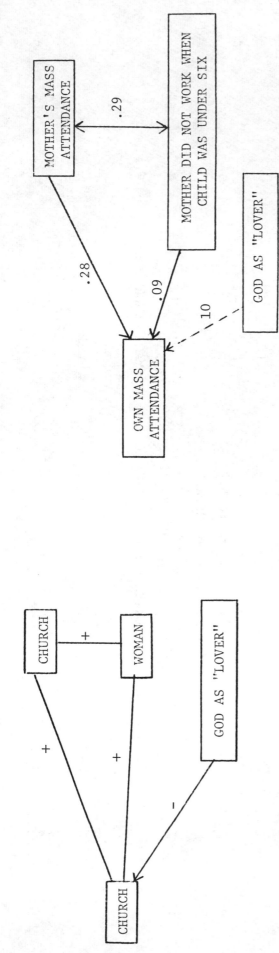

A) HYPOTHESIZED RELATIONSHIPS

B) ACTUAL RELATIONSHIPS

FIGURE 3.3

RELATIONSHIP AMONG IMAGES FOR "TRADITIONAL" WOMEN

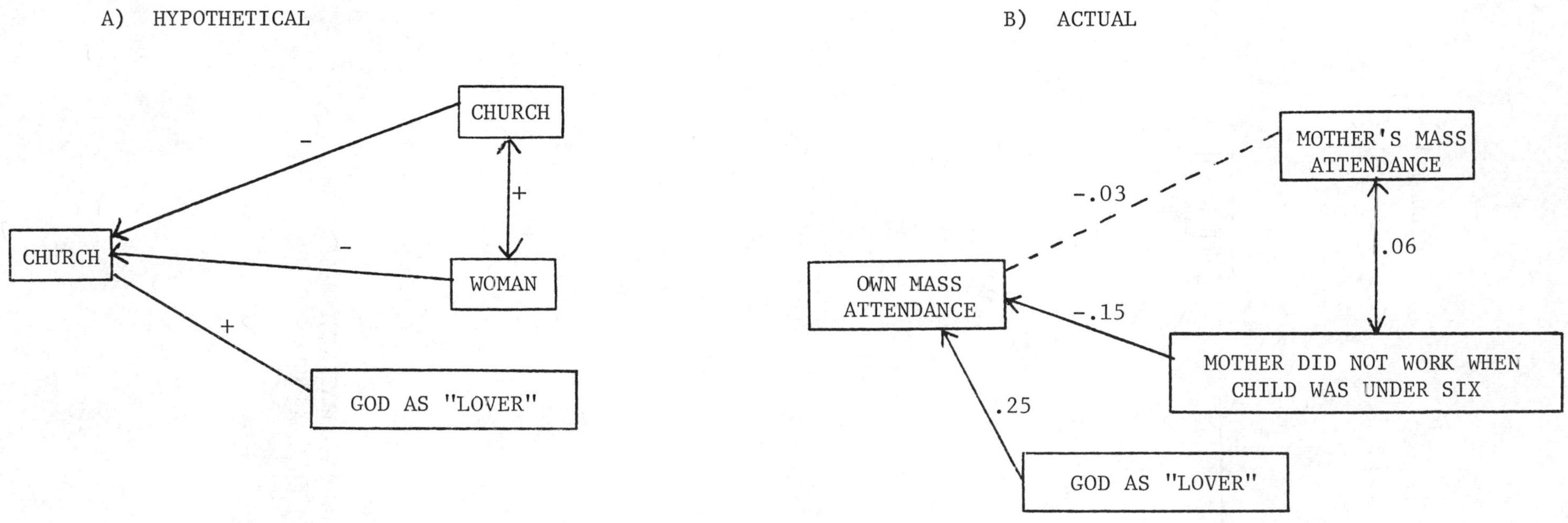

207

A) HYPOTHETICAL

B) ACTUAL

FIGURE 3.4

RELATIONSHIP AMONG IMAGES FOR "FEMINIST" WOMEN

NOW   CHILDHOOD

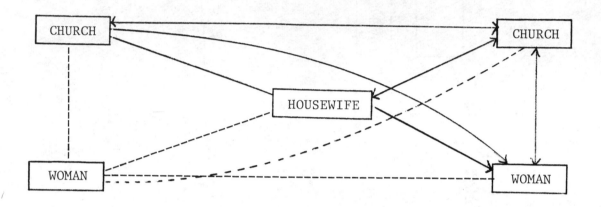

——— Positive

- - - - Negative

FIGURE 4.1

SELF-IMAGE AS HOUSEWIFE REINFORCING INCOMPATIBILITY BETWEEN
IMAGE OF WOMAN AND IMAGE OF CHURCH

FIGURE 6.1

INVERTED TREE MODEL FOR RELATIONSHIP BETWEEN CHURCH ATTENDANCE AND FEMINISM

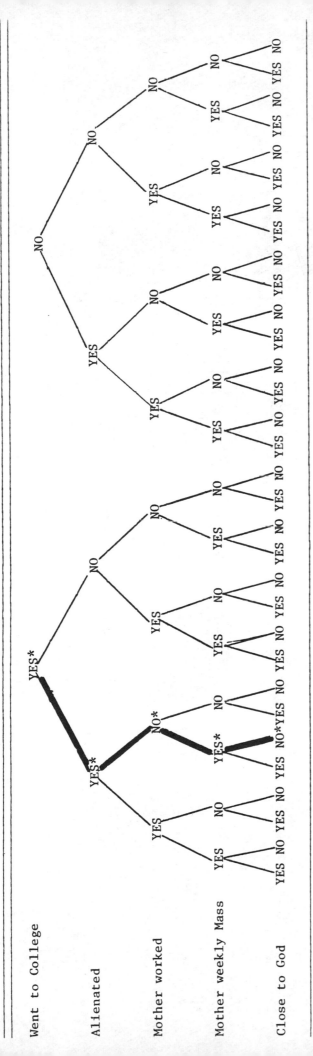

*Only branches on which there is a statistically significant relationship between "feminism" and church attendance for Catholic women. All other branches are N.S. (Not Significant).

210

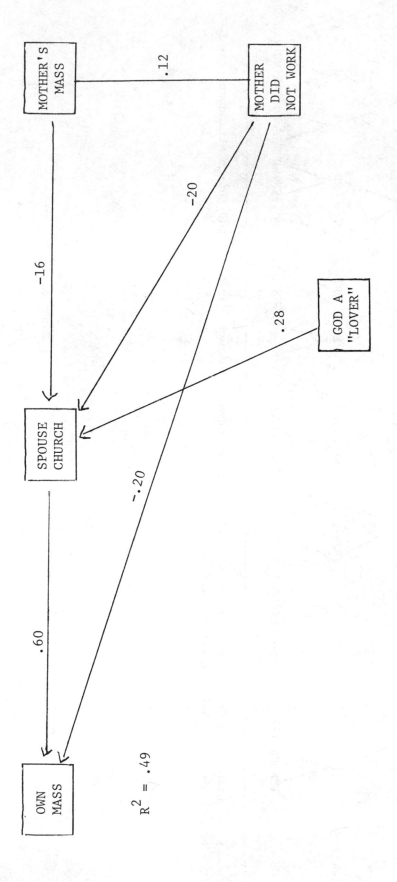

FIGURE 7.1: FEMINISTS

211

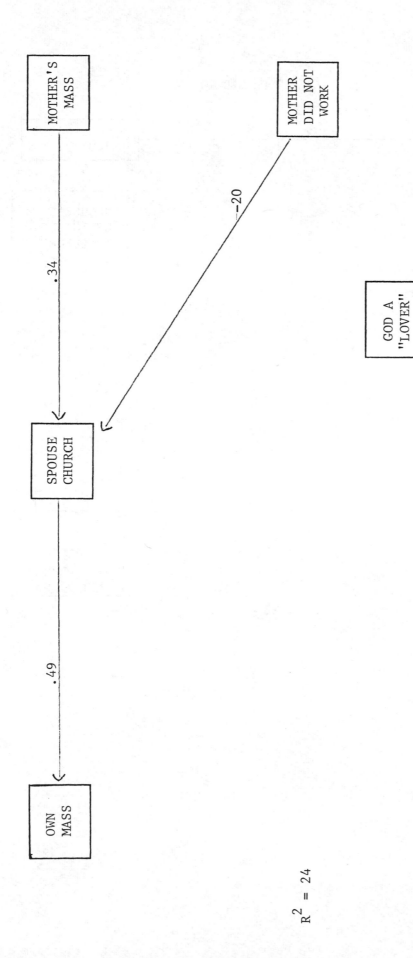

FIGURE 7.2:   TRADITIONALISTS

7.3

A) FEMINIST WOMEN

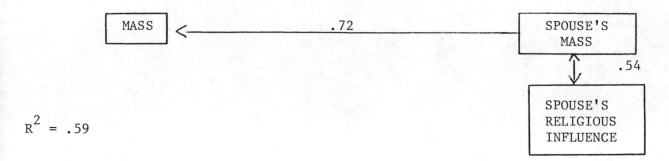

R^2 = .59

B) TRADITIONAL WOMEN

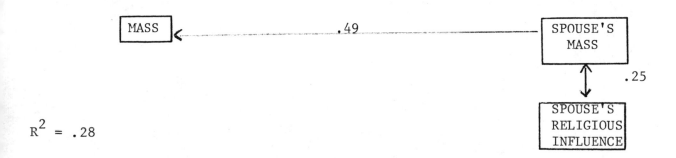

R^2 = .28

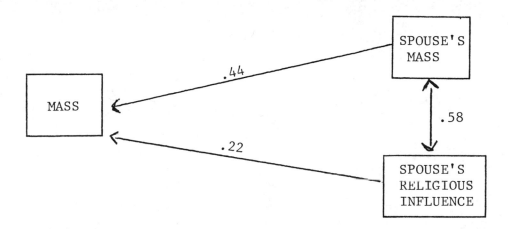

$R^2 = .60$

7.4:   FEMINIST WOMEN WHOSE HUSBANDS ARE FEMINIST